COMPUTER SCIENCE

AN ILLUSTRATED HISTORY OF
THE WORLD'S SMARTEST MACHINES

PONDERABLES™

100 Achievements That Changed History

WHO DID WHAT WHEN

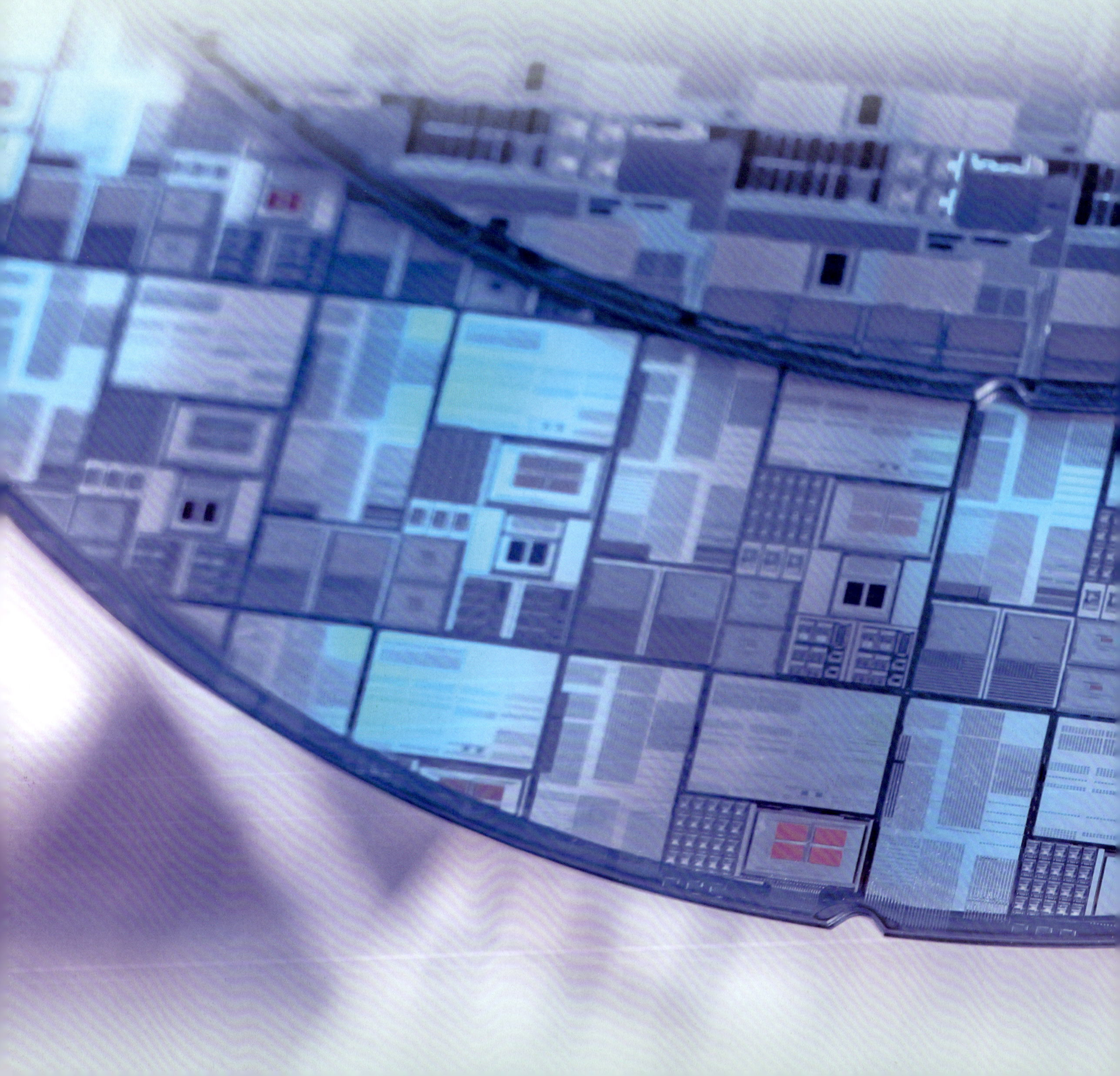

COMPUTER SCIENCE

AN ILLUSTRATED HISTORY OF THE WORLD'S SMARTEST MACHINES

Tom Jackson

Shelter Harbor Press
NEW YORK

Contents

INTRODUCTION 6

1	The Abacus	10
2	The Antikythera Mechanism	11
3	The Aztec Computer	12
4	The Astrolabe	13
5	Inventing Zero	13
6	Clockwork	14
7	Napier's Logarithmic Bones	15
8	The Pascaline Calculator	15
9	Binary Code	16
10	Automata	18
11	Punched Card Programs	19
12	The Analytical Engine	20
13	Wired Telecoms	22
14	Software	23
15	Algorithms	24
16	Analog Computers	26
17	The Keyboard	27
18	Voice Networks	28
19	Hollerith's Tabulator	29
20	Human Computers	30

21	Wireless Communication	31
22	Thermionic Valve	31
23	Robots	32
24	Display Screens	34
25	Vannevar Bush	35
26	The Turing Machine	36
27	Using Logic	38
28	Enigma Code	40
29	The First Network	42
30	Colossus, the First of Billions	42
31	ENIAC: The Giant Electronic Brain	43
32	Finding Bugs	44
33	The Transistor	44
34	Information Theory	46
35	The Turing Test	47
36	Compilers	48
37	Mainframes	48
38	Memory and Storage	50
39	Fortran	51
40	How To Be a Real Hacker	52
41	The Perceptron	53
42	Inventing the Microchip	54
43	Computer Modelling	56
44	Moore's Law	57
45	UNIX	57
46	Switching On the Internet	58
47	Email	60
48	Malware	60
49	Broadcasting Text	62

50	The GUI	62
51	The Homebrew Computer Club	64
52	Microcomputer	65
53	Supercomputer	65
54	The Atari 2600	66
55	How Do Touchscreens Work?	67
56	Encryption: The Basics	68
57	The Origins of AI	70
58	Laptops	72
59	Personal Computers	72
60	Computer-Generated Imagery	74
61	Open Source Software	75
62	Optical Fibers	76
63	Self-Driving Cars	76
64	Printing for All	78
65	MS Office	79
66	The World Wide Web	80
67	Bluetooth	82
68	GPS Navigation	82
69	Virtual Reality	84
70	E-Commerce	85
71	Chess Computer	86
72	The Optical Disc	87
73	E-ink	87
74	Search Engines	88
75	Wi-Fi	90
76	iPod	91
77	Hactivism	92
78	Video Calling	93
79	Social Media	94
80	Data Mining	96
81	Smartphone	97
82	Gig Economy	98
83	Wearables	99
84	Cryptocurrency	100
85	Watson, the Quiz AI	102
86	Cloud Computing	102
87	Machine Learning	104
88	Biometrics	106
89	Near-Field Technology	107
90	Smart Speakers	107
91	Haptics	108
92	The DARPA Robotics Challenge	108
93	Data Protection	110
94	Quantum Computing	110
95	Big Data	112
96	Internet of Things	112
97	NFTs	114
98	A Brain Interface	114
99	AlphaFold	115
100	Generative AI	116

Computer Science 101: The basics	118
Imponderables	124
The Great Computer Scientists	132
Bibliography and Other Resources	140
Index	141
Acknowledgments	144

A Timeline History of Computer Science	Back
History of the Modern Computer	pocket

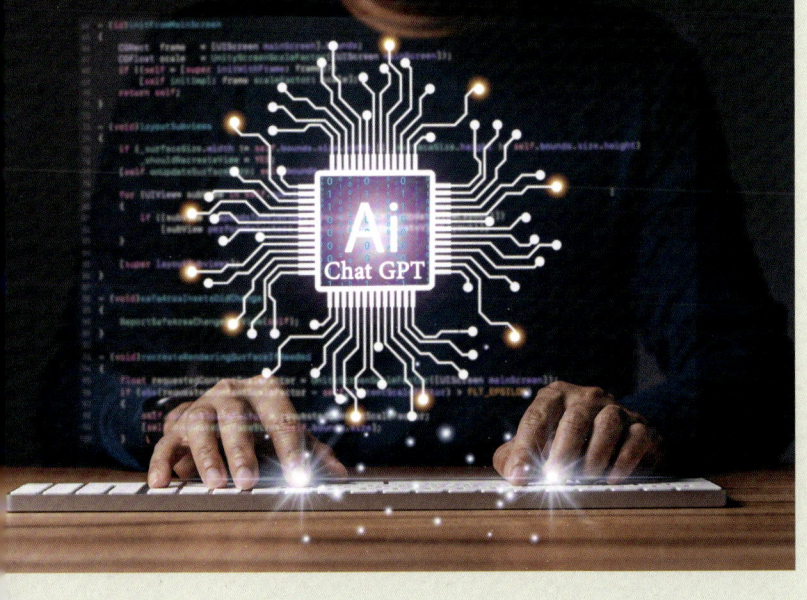

Introduction

Computer scientists are the people of the moment. As we stand on the verge of an AI revolution, where artificial intelligence is poised to change our lives (for the better or worse), it is computer science that got us here and will determine what happens next. Perhaps there is no more important topic right now. There is much to know, so let's get started.

Take a step back a minute and look at computing in terms of a few numbers. The first computers were built around 70 years ago, at a rate of about one a year to start with. Today, there are two billion computers sitting on desks and in homes around the world—one for every four people. However, those computers are just a fraction of the 17 billion computing devices connected to the Internet today—a number that is set to double by the 2030s. And what do all these devices, which also include phones, tablets, and smart gadgets of all kinds, have in common? They are using semiconducting transistors to control their processes and perform their functions. In total, it is estimated that to date, 13 sextillion transistors (that's 13 with 21 zeros) have been manufactured, making them—by some margin—the most abundant artificial item on Earth.

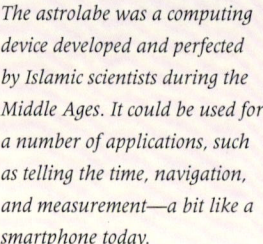

The astrolabe was a computing device developed and perfected by Islamic scientists during the Middle Ages. It could be used for a number of applications, such as telling the time, navigation, and measurement—a bit like a smartphone today.

The Hollerith Tabulating Machine from the 1890s automated the analysis of U.S. census data. The electromechanical machine demonstrated the power of computing, and its inventor went on to be a founding figure in International Business Machines, or IBM, the first giant computing company.

Not bad for an object measuring a few billionths of a meter in length and essentially manufactured from refined sand! It will come as no surprise that the story of computer science has many characters who contribute to this considerable sum. The story of the world's most complex devices is itself filled with complexity, but the big picture is a compelling one. And here we tell it in 100 steps, starting in ancient days, when calculators were based on beads and counters, and computers were actually people. Where it ends is unwritten. One day, this story may get updated and be written on a computer itself. Right now, though, it is us humans that will decide the plot twists. What do you think should happen next?

LUCKY OR CLEVER?

The computer—at least one that is workable—was created by accident, not quite by design. That is not to say that people failed to recognize long ago that a computing machine was nothing but a good idea. Civilization is a human project. It is about us humans building systems that take control of the natural world, so we can live longer (and happier) lives in ever larger groups. It's a work in progress as much today as it ever was, but as civilizations accrued property, possessions, and knowledge, the data sets that came along with them began to outgrow human comprehension. We build recording systems to remember it all for us. The earliest writings are often lists of who owns what, but they were soon recording things like the location of stars or telling stories and poems. Extracting useful information from these records was getting harder, so devices were built for computing the numbers. By computing, we mean applying a set of operations (things like adding or multiplying) to the numbers, so they are processed into an answer. The abacus was an early computing device. It worked so well that mechanical upgrades were only attempted in the last few centuries, with mixed results. However, in the end, the system that resulted in the

INTRODUCTION * 7

modern computer was not created to meet our needs of crunching data. Instead, it was a thought experiment conjured in the head of Alan Turing. His "virtual machine" could do any set of operations, no matter what the order or purpose. Turing created it to solve a big problem in mathematics, but then realized that if his machine was made for real, it could be a universal computing device. It could perform any job, as long as we gave it the right instructions.

MEETING NEEDS, OLD AND NEW

And so began the process of figuring out what instructions to give it. The physical device, or computer hardware, was enhanced to follow instructions faster and so outstrip the abilities of humans for speed and accuracy many times over. The instructions that followed were for the software; so-called "soft" because it is a non-physical component of computing. As you will see on the following pages, this endeavor has had some remarkable results, with every decade or so marking a new revolutionary way that computing can be used. In the 1960s, computers were the engines of commerce, deployed by large organizations to handle data on a grand scale. Next, computing became distributed, with individuals working on their own personal computers. Here, the software instructions were cast to meet the user's needs: Writing documents, analyzing data, and storing information. And when the work was done, it became a machine for playing games. What next? Just the World Wide Web. The Web democratized computing. The computer moved away from a serious tool and became a device for creating and consuming "content." That could be entertainment or news (or a mash-up of the two), or simply gossip and chats between friends—and perhaps also with trolls, who were less friendly.

One of the most successful forms of artificial intelligence is the kind that is trained to do jobs in a process called machine learning. This involves finding patterns in jumbled data.

Spot is a robotic dog. Its advanced motors, battery, cameras, and other sensors create an agile machine that can walk almost anywhere. Its AI systems make it autonomous enough to work alone, explore remote locations searching for problems, or monitor machinery.

CLEVER OR DUMB?

In all this time, computer science has been looking for a special set of software instructions—ones that allow the computer to behave in intelligent ways. Artificial intelligence (AI) is able to carry out a set of complex tasks with no input from us. It took longer than we expected, but a technique called generative AI appears to meet our expectations of what AI should be capable of. This AI may one day constitute a computer "mind" that thinks ahead and makes plans—something we humans excel at. Many of the smartest people in the room (some of whom built the AI) are urging that we all think ahead and make plans about what happens next. What should AI be allowed to do, and how do we ensure it stays under our control? One thing is certain: We are heading for an AI future, and to understand that better, a good place is to look back into the past at the whole story of computer science. Let's begin!

COMPUTER ARCHITECTURE

There would appear to be little in common between a vast mainframe computer, with its forest of wire and hot, glowing vacuum tubes, and a smartwatch or phone in your pocket. However, they all use the same basic architecture. This was developed at the dawn of modern computing as a way of making Turing's "virtual machine" real. Despite the different looks, all computers from the 1950s have four kinds of device: input, output, and storage—all connected to the central processing unit.

DATA FLOW   CONTROL

INPUT

1 INPUT DEVICES

This is where data enters the computer. It can be an active device, with a human user busily typing words on a keyboard (hello there!) or clicking on a mouse. As computers integrate further with our apparel and built environment, these active input devices become less obvious. A smart speaker's primary input is the microphone listening for your voice, while swiping and tapping on a smartwatch touchscreen is the main way to input data there. There are other passive input devices, such as motion detectors and cameras that input data without you having to operate them. Wherever the source of the data is, it heads to the central processing unit.

Mouse
A handheld device for moving a cursor across the screen and clicking on target items.

Camera
The pattern of light entering the camera is converted to digital code.

Light Sensor
Light hitting the sensor alters its conductivity and so creates a signal that indicates light and dark.

Musical Instrument
The player's keystrokes are converted into a digital signal.

Keyboard
Combinations of keystrokes create codes specific to a letter or other character.

Touchscreen
A fingertip changes the conductivity of the screen wherever it touches.

Rain Sensor
Water hitting the device alters the conductivity, creating a signal when it rains.

Data Glove
The motion of the hand is transmitted to the computer. It can also act as an output device.

Scanner
Light reflecting off a photo or document creates a pattern that is converted to digital code.

Microphone
Sound waves vibrate a magnetic sensor that converts the sound into an electrical wave, which is then digitized.

Motion Sensor
The sensor is able to detect changes in infrared radiation (heat). A moving person creates a signal.

The Web
This can be viewed as an input device. Streaming data, web pages, and other content all comes from the Web. The Web serves as a storage and output device as well!

CENTRAL PROCESSING UNIT

- CONTROL UNIT
- ARITHMETIC AND LOGIC UNIT
- MEMORY

STORAGE

OUTPUT

2 CENTRAL PROCESSING UNIT

The flow of data around the CPU and between other devices is the job of the control unit. It pulls in the program's instructions brought in from storage, and carries out the requisite tasks by sending commands to the other components in the CPU. Essentially, the tasks require a logical operation or a piece of math, and this is the job of the arithmetic and logic unit. The results are held in several fast-acting memory units, called registers. This is where the live data that the CPU needs right now is being stored. There are specific registers in the CPU for different kinds of code and data. The registers are there to allow the CPU to run as fast as possible. Extra data is sent and received by the RAM (random access memory). Once processed, the data from the CPU is sent to an output device.

Internal Hard Drive
A magnetic disc that stores data long-term. Becoming less common.

Optical Disc
Data is stored as patterns of reflective sectors.

The Cloud
Data can be stored in computers connected via the Web—for a fee.

External Hard Drive
A cheap and reliable way of increasing storage capacity.

Solid State Memory
A more compact storage system based on microchip technology.

Monitor
Also called a display, this outputs information as an image on a screen.

Smartphone
The phone has both a screen and a speaker.

Television
The main screen in the house can be used as a computer output.

Loudspeaker
Turn it up! The wobbling cone creates sound waves.

Headphones
Smaller speakers that are designed for private listening.

Printer
A coded pattern is converted to a physical copy using inks on paper.

3D Printer
Builds up layers of plastic to make a solid object.

Electric Vehicle Motor
This power system is controlled by a computer.

Drone
These flying machines require computer control.

The Web
Sending messages and sharing photos makes the Web an output device.

4 STORAGE DEVICES

This fourth type of device is not entirely necessary. For example, a washing machine is a computer with input, processor, and output, but it has no storage option. However, a computer always has storage. It is there to hold data long-term. It is a digital filing cabinet, memory box, photo album, music collection… the list is endless, although the storage is not! The terms storage and memory are easily confused. Memory is better understood as the RAM working with the CPU. However, the storage can be used as an overflow option for this purpose. When your computer is running slowly, it may be because data is moving back and forth from its internal storage. Modern computers use solid-state memory as standard, which is faster at this kind of thing.

3 OUTPUT DEVICES

This is the bit you've been waiting for—literally. The inputted data has been processed into useful information by the CPU. Whatever you have asked the computer to do, the information you require is delivered to an output device. The most obvious is the display or monitor, but outputs can be sounds, printed hard copies, or even a robotic device like a drone or electric vehicle.

1 The Abacus

IF A COMPUTER AT ITS SIMPLEST IS A DEVICE FOR PROCESSING DATA, then an abacus goes some way to meeting that description. And this computing machine is 4,500 years old!

It is not that many years since it was common in parts of East Asia to see storekeepers use an abacus (the plural is "abaci") to tally the price of goods with an impressive speed. In other parts of the world, the cashier might have used pen and paper to add up the prices, but that new-fangled technique was only widely introduced 500 years ago! For many, the old-fashioned abacus was enough. It had worked perfectly well for more than a millennium. Now, of course, no human is doing these calculations at all. Instead, a laser scanner identifies each product, a total is summed, and the money is transferred, all by computer.

The abacus is a counting frame that works like a computing machine because it can accept inputs by moving counters. It can store numbers using the position of the counters, and finally it can output the answer to a calculation. The frame limits the "programs" that can be followed, but abaci can be used for a range of operations over and above just adding and subtracting, and they can handle different bases.

> **CALCULATING BEGINS**
> Stone Age humans had calculators: The words "calculate" and "calculator" come from *calx*, the Latin word for "stone." Small stones, or pebbles, were *calculi*, and were used as counters in ancient times. One scenario was a shepherd counting the flock each morning by making a pile of stones—one pebble for every sheep. If, by the evening, the number of pebbles did not match the number of sheep, the shepherd knew how many more animals he needed to go and find. The one-to-one means of tallying quantities was upgraded in the earliest civilizations, such as Uruk (in what is now Iraq). Here, quantities were represented by clay tokens that were sealed in round clay balls.

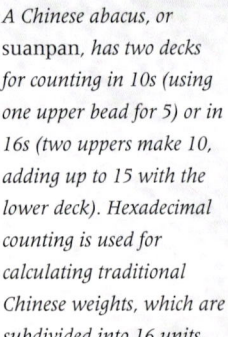

A Chinese abacus, or suanpan, *has two decks for counting in 10s (using one upper bead for 5) or in 16s (two uppers make 10, adding up to 15 with the lower deck). Hexadecimal counting is used for calculating traditional Chinese weights, which are subdivided into 16 units.*

A global success

The familiar counting-frame abacus is perhaps not quite as ancient as it might be imagined. It is a fusion of the counting tables developed in the Near East, with the counting rods of the Far East. The word *abacus* derives from Arabic for "dust," which probably alludes to a sandy pit with columns of pebbles or other counters. In China, the counters were stacked on rods, a bit like a toddler's puzzle. Chinese numerals from around the 3rd century BCE resembled upright rods with stacks of disks. It was not until the 16th century CE that the two approaches were combined into a handy frame.

2 The Antikythera Mechanism

SALVAGED FROM A SHIP THAT SANK IN THE AEGEAN SEA 2,100 YEARS AGO, this set of corroded bronze dials is regarded as a primordial computing device. There is nothing else like it from the ancient world.

Discovered on the seabed in 1901 just off the coast of Antikythera, a small island near Crete, the device was causing a stir before it even reached the surface. It was part of a jumble of cargo made up of bronze and marble statues and a variety of other treasures muddled in with everyday items like wine jugs and furniture. The ship had been carrying a Roman general back to Italy, and he had filled the hold with a variety of loot plundered from Athens. Then it sank and lay undiscovered until sponge divers came across it in 1900. The following summer, attempts were made to raise the artefacts. In 198 feet (60 m) of water, this meant divers working at the limit of the equipment of the day. One diver died and two others were paralyzed by decompression sickness before the salvage expedition was ended.

Fragment A of the mechanism has cogs either side of a piece of wood. There was an unknown number of gears that were lost, along with the handle that cranked the device.

Precision construction

The following year, an archaeologist came across several fragments of cogs placed on wooden boards. To the untrained eyes of the divers this was an interesting piece of ancient clockwork, but the archaeologist knew that this technology was unheard of from the 1st century BCE. The precision craftsmanship of the mechanism, where the teeth of the cogs fit together well enough to work as gears, was centuries ahead of itself.

During a painstaking process of cleaning and reconstruction, it was suggested that the mechanism was an analog computing device—ie it gave a simulation or analog of real-world events. The panels indicated that the original device was built around a box. The mechanism is so precise that there must have been several earlier versions. Experts surmise that the gadget originally came from Rhodes, the home of Hipparchus, a famous astronomer. The leading theory goes that the gears are part of a larger mechanical computer based on the observations of the Sun and Moon, made by Hipparchus. Turning the device altered dials on the front face that indicated the positions of the Sun, the phases of the Moon and—perhaps—the locations of the planets against the zodiac.

3 The Aztec Computer

INNOVATION IN COMPUTING DEVICES WAS NOT CONFINED TO THE "OLD WORLD" of Europe and Asia. However, the counting and calculation devices of Pre-Conquest America did things a little differently.

Around the turn of the 2nd millennium CE there appeared to be a remarkable match up of computing systems on both sides of the Pacific Ocean. In China the abacus, or *suanpan*, was taking hold as the go-to calculating machine. Meanwhile, in the pre-Columbian civilizations of Central America a similar device was in use.

Today the device is sometimes called the Aztec Computer, but this belies its provenance. It is proposed that the ancient Olmec people invented it as long as 3,000 years ago, and it was later improved by the Maya. The device was like an abacus with dried maize kernels threaded as beads on strings. It was based on a five-digit vigesimal or base-20 counting system.

Smart device

Around the 11th century CE, the Aztecs innovated the device further. They knew it as the *nepohualtzintzin*, which means "relevant counter." Although no original "nepo" survives, it is thought that it was worn on the wrist as an elaborate bracelet. The device had 91 beads in 13 horizontal rows. The left side of each row had four beads (1 to 4), while the right had three (to count 5, 10, and 15). It could be used as a base-20 abacus, but with that number of rows, the numbers grow to quantities seemingly impractical for everyday life. Instead, the setup suggests that the *nepohualtzintzin* was as much a calendar as it was a calculator. One nepo (91) represented the days of a season, twice through the nepo (182) was the number of days from sowing corn to harvesting it. Four nepos (364) marked a full year (more or less).

This is a replica of a 1470s sculpture called the sun stone. It is a representation of the Universe as seen by the Aztecs. The Aztec computer, or nepohualtzintzin, was used to keep track of the seasons or the year, and its immense calculating power may have been used to work with the complex multi-cycle calendars of Mesoamerican civilization.

MAYAN COUNTING

The Mayan numeral system independently arrived at a symbol for zero, possibly before it became a feature of math over in the "Old World." The Mayan system used three symbols: A dot or pebble shape represented 1, a stick showed 5, and the shell was used for zero. They used base 20, so that number was written as a pebble at the top to signify 1 x 20, and then a shell beneath indicated zero units.

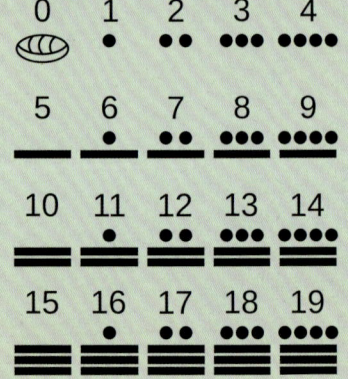

4 The Astrolabe

BY THE 10TH CENTURY, THE WORLD CENTER OF LEARNING had swung to Baghdad, at the heart of the Islamic empire. Here, the astrolabe, literally a "star taker," emerged as a combination of beauty and high tech.

The astrolabe is thought to have had its roots in an ancient Greek instrument—perhaps something like the Antikythera Mechanism. However, it reached its full potential in the hands of Islamic scientists. It was nevertheless later superseded by the sextant and mechanical watch—and then the smartphone!

In the way its components were calibrated to work together and generate outputs from input, the astrolabe was very much an analog computer. In fact, it could be said that the astrolabe was the smartphone of the medieval world. It was a series of overlaid metal discs that connected in the center. They turned independently of each other to line up a variety of concentric dials and symbols. It could be made small enough to carry in a pocket, but, as with a smartphone, the bigger ones were easier to use across their wide range of functions. The astrolabe was essentially an astronomical tool that used the motion of the heavens to work as a calendar, clock, and navigational aid. It could also be used to make measurements of the position of stars and planets above the horizon or relative to each other.

5 Inventing Zero

MODERN COMPUTING IS DIGITAL—AT LEAST FOR NOW—and that means it works using digits, or numbers. In fact, it only needs two numbers, 1 and 0. The number 1 did not need inventing, but zero definitely did.

Counting comes naturally to us—up to a point. Our most distant early human ancestors would have had an eye on the quantities of important things—livestock, children, friends (but maybe not in that order). It is less natural for us to measure and record nothing as a quantity, but that is exactly what digital computing requires. And long before that, the concept of nothing was required by the burgeoning civilizations as they invented money, collected tax, and created debts—or negative quantities of things. (A negative number is anything less than zero.) So where did zero come from?

What we now understand as a zero first appears in Babylonian numbers as a pair of angled wedges. This zero represents an absence of a value within a larger number. (In 404, the zero stands for the absence of any tens in the number.) This type of zero turned up independently in Mayan numbers, but elsewhere in the ancient world mathematics did not require zero. In the 3rd century CE (or perhaps before) Indian mathematicians made zero into a number like any other by simply showing that some expressions produced zero as the answer. Now the stage was set for the 1s and 0s of digital code. It just needed a few more centuries of advances in other technologies first.

6 Clockwork

A CLOCK DOES NOT MEASURE TIME. IT IS NOT DETECTING the flow of time passing. Instead it is computing periods of time using the inputs from a reliable oscillation, such as a pendulum. Early mechanical computers used different inputs, but still made use of the same intricate clockwork.

This water-powered Chinese clock tower dates from the 11th century CE. The flow of water through the wheel inside turned various astronomical devices that modelled the motion of the heavens. The clock was used as much for timing divination and rituals as it was for scientific enquiry.

The first clocks relied on physical processes to keep time. The sundial was simply showing the position of the Sun in the sky as it progressed from dawn till dusk. Water clocks and sand timers relied on the pull of gravity to empty a container in the same amount of time. But then the clock had to be reset. The same was true of candle or lamp clocks used in temples and churches, which burned away hour after hour. The innovation needed was a mechanical oscillator that would run by itself once given a source of energy. In the 13th century, weight-driven mechanical timekeepers were being installed in churches and cathedrals across Europe. The weight pulled on clockwork with the required force, so that they turned every hour (or other time period). Each cycle culminated in the striking of a bell, or *clocca* in Church Latin—hence the word "clock." The pendulum proved to be a more reliable oscillator, as shown by Galileo Galilei in the late 16th century. It was the Dutch astronomer Christiaan Huygens who devised the first pendulum clock in 1656. As with every preceding step, this clock relied on ever more precise craftsmanship, so the mechanisms transmitted motion exactly. The mass production of brass that began in the 1740s was another significant change. Brass, an alloy of copper and zinc, is easy enough to work into intricate cogs and gears, but is hard and corrosion resistant. As clocks became smaller, the brass clockwork encouraged innovators to think big. What else could these well-oiled devices be used for?

7 Napier's Logarithmic Bones

THIS DEVICE ALLOWED SOMEONE to make perform tricky mathematical operations without understanding them.

Napier's bones were akin to a portable set of multiplication tables.

To the modern user this sounds all too familiar, but the device, named for John Napier, an eccentric Scottish mathematician, was the first of its kind. It is a set of ten rods covered in spirals of numbers. The rods could be turned to set an input value, and then the device converted a long multiplication or other arithmetic operation into a simpler sum or subtraction. Napier's "bones," invented in the 16th century, was the precursor of the slide-rule, which did much the same job until the dawn of the computer age.

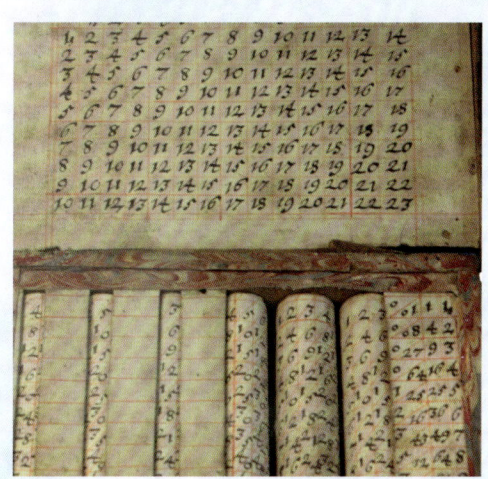

8 The Pascaline Calculator

THE WORD *COMPUTER* HAILS FROM 1613. It meant a person who did complex calculations. So why not make a machine that does the same thing?

Numbers of up to six digits were inputted to the Pascaline by turning the dials. Inputting a second number results in it being added to the first one.

Blaise Pascal's father was a computer. He was busy reorganizing the tax system of a French province. The young Blaise saw the advantage of having an automatic calculator to help with this task, and in 1642—at the age of just 19—he began to develop what became the Pascaline, the first mechanical calculator. He built 50 versions before perfecting the device. Nine working Pascalines survive. Society never looked back. Today, everything from a cash register to a spreadsheet does the math for us.

The Pascaline was built for adding, but it could be switched to subtraction mode using a lever. Multiplication was achieved by repeated additions. Numbers were dialed in by turning wheels and each digit appeared in windows above. If the result required it, a figure was carried to the next column by a system of gears and escapements not dissimilar to the workings of a clock.

9 Binary Code

THE WORD *DIGITAL* IS OFTEN A PRECURSOR IN THE DESCRIPTION OF THE LATEST TECHNOLOGY. It really just means "using numbers," and more often than not just two numbers, 0 and 1. Welcome to the binary system.

Whether we realize it or not we are all intensely familiar with the decimal system of counting, where we use ten numerals—0 to 9—as the units. Above that value we start to count in 10s and then 100s. Binary is a positional counting system that uses just two numerals. That means the number two is written 10 and four is 100. This seems like more trouble than it's worth, but binary has its uses.

The representation of the binary system set out by Leibniz in this 1703 publication of his paper Explication de l'Arithmétique Binaire, *is basically the one used today.*

Ones and zeros

The benefit of binary is most apparent in the spooky world of codes and cyberspace. This was spotted by a remarkably prescient Francis Bacon in 1605. Bacon was a founding figure in all kinds of fields, not least in codifying the Scientific Method, which helped usher in the Scientific Revolution of the 17th century. He also had a hand in identifying the way binary could be used to transmit information.

Bacon ciphered all 26 letters of the English alphabet using strings of five binary characters. There are 26 letters and the total permutations of five characters is 32 (2^5). Bacon's cipher used *a*'s and *b*'s rather than numerals. Another science superstar

I CHING

Gottfried Leibniz was an avid orientalist, endlessly fascinated with what he regarded as the mysterious East. Just like many similarly minded people after him would, his research took in the *I Ching*, one of the oldest works of Chinese literature, dating from 1000 BCE, if not before. It purports to be a means of predicting the future and uses a series of symbols called trigrams and hexagrams. The eight trigrams—the ones often seen arranged around the *yinyang* symbol—are made of three lines, while the 64 hexagrams (right) have six lines. An unbroken line represents *yang*, a broken one is *yin*, opposite parts of an interconnected whole: Leibniz saw them as something more—binary 0s and 1s. That gave the hexagrams a numerical value up to 2^6 (64). The trigrams counted up to 2^3 (8). Hexagrams are in effect doubled trigrams ($2^3 \times 2^3 = 2^6$).

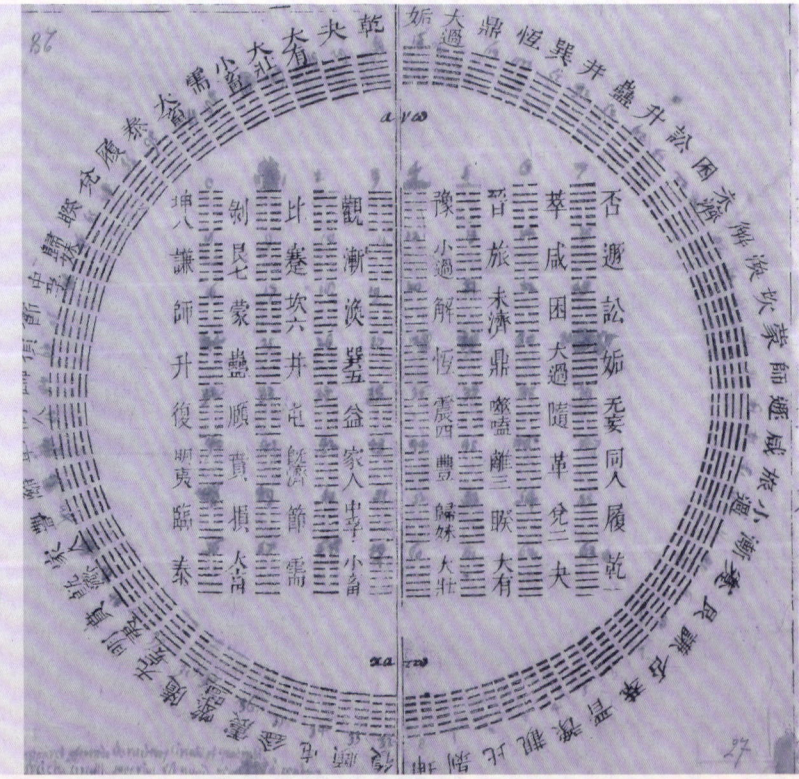

PREHISTORY TO 1900 CE * 17

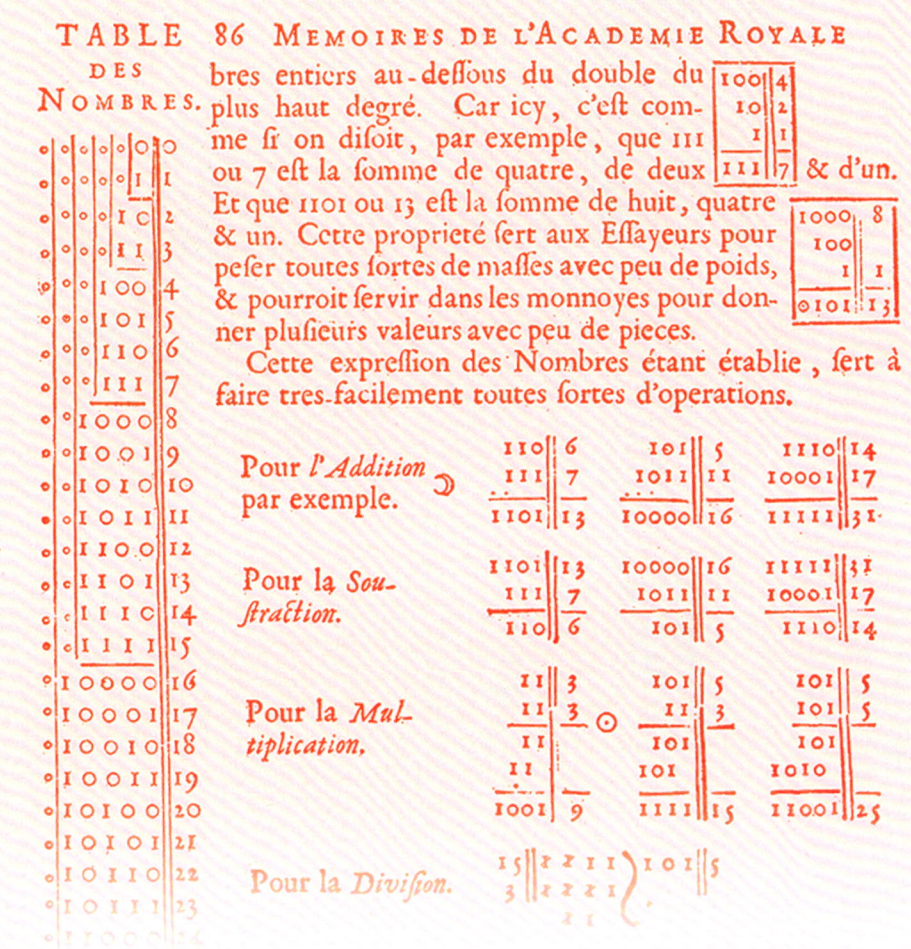

HEXADECIMAL

After 10 and 2, the base that is most in use is 16. This is used to create hexadecimal, or hex, codes. The 16 numerals are 0 to F. As the table below shows, the decimal number 15 is simplified to F in hex. Using letters as numerals gives the chance to spell some words. FACE is 64206 in decimal and 1111101011001110 in binary. The role of hexadecimal is to simplify, or at least truncate, binary numbers, which can become unwieldy at best —as the above example illustrates well. A common place one might see hexademical is in the passwords used to connect to home Wi-Fi routers. If you have some spare time (perhaps a lot) you could convert that passcode into decimal and binary.

Binary	Decimal	Hex
0000	0	0
0001	1	1
0010	2	2
0011	3	3
0100	4	4
0101	5	5
0110	6	6
0111	7	7
1000	8	8
1001	9	9
1010	10	A
1011	11	B
1100	12	C
1101	13	D
1110	14	E
1111	15	F

created the current binary notation. Gottfried Leibniz, one of the founders of calculus, introduced the 0 and 1 digits in his *Explanation of Binary Arithmetic*, published in 1679. While it requires a good deal of practice to read binary numbers, Leibniz set them out in the same way as any decimal number.

Read right to left, the first figure of a decimal number, let's say 31, is the units (1), and the next is the number of tens (3). Decimal numbers continue into the hundreds, thousands, and so on. Each additional number position is 10 to the next power: The units are multiples of 10^0, which equals 1, the tens are 10^1, hundreds are 10^2, and thousands 10^3. The binary system merely replaces 10 with 2. The number begins with the units: 2^0 or multiples of 1. The next position is 2^1, which is simply 2 in decimal but 10 in binary. The positions that follow are 2^2, 2^3, 2^4, which are 4s, 8s, and 16s. So ending where we began, the decimal number 31 is the binary number 11111.

Two-state solutions

Francis Bacon had already taken the concept further. He also saw that the letters could be transmitted by any method with a "twofold difference only; as by Bells, by Trumpets, by Lights and Torches, by the report of Muskets, and any instruments of like nature." Two centuries later, Samuel Morse's telegraph code of dots and dashes certainly owes a debt to this notion, as does the modern world. What are the switch-like transistors of a microprocessor if not just such a *twofold instrument*.

10 Automata

ANOTHER ROUTE TO COMPUTING IS OUR DRIVE TO AUTOMATE. Since time immemorial we have imagined machines that can do our work for us. Automata were early attempts at exploring, often in a fun way, how this might come to pass.

Perhaps the most significant automaton was the Digesting Duck. This device was constructed by Jacques de Vaucanson and revealed to the French public in 1764. It was a common theme that automata copied natural bodies and movements, and this model took that to its logical conclusion. The copper bird would stoop to swallow grains of wheat, flap its wings, and then expel a spherical dropping! If the Digesting Duck could perform the basics of life, what limits were there? As it turned out, there were many.

Master craftsman

In the 1st century CE, Heron of Alexandria, the inventor of a primitive steam engine, had imagined a staff of mechanical servants powered by his device. However, his tools let him down. He nevertheless managed a vending machine that delivered water in return for a coin.

Ismail al-Jazari, a 12th-century engineer, is known as the father of robotics, thanks to his many lifelike automata. For example, he built a waitress that slid out through automatic doors to deliver a drink on a tray. Today's automata are still basically dispensers and vending machines. What they lack, just as Heron's and al-Jazari's devices did, is autonomy, or the ability to alter what they do. This technology gap is only just being filled now with artificial intelligence. Will Heron's dream come true?

In 1495, Leonardo da Vinci, famed in our time for painting the Mona Lisa, *sketched plans for the Mechanical Knight. Recreated here, this was meant to be an armored robot that moved all by itself. The great artist copied the structure of the human body to make the mechanical joints.*

AL-JAZARI
This ingenious engineer lived in what is now Diyarbakir, southeastern Turkey. His job was to maintain the royal palace, but he added a few mechanical extras. These used the technology of the time and were mechanisms of cogs, pistons, and chain drives, all powered by hidden water wheels. In 1206 he recorded his designs, including the one for the water-powered elephant clock (above), in *The Book of Knowledge of Ingenious Mechanical Devices*.

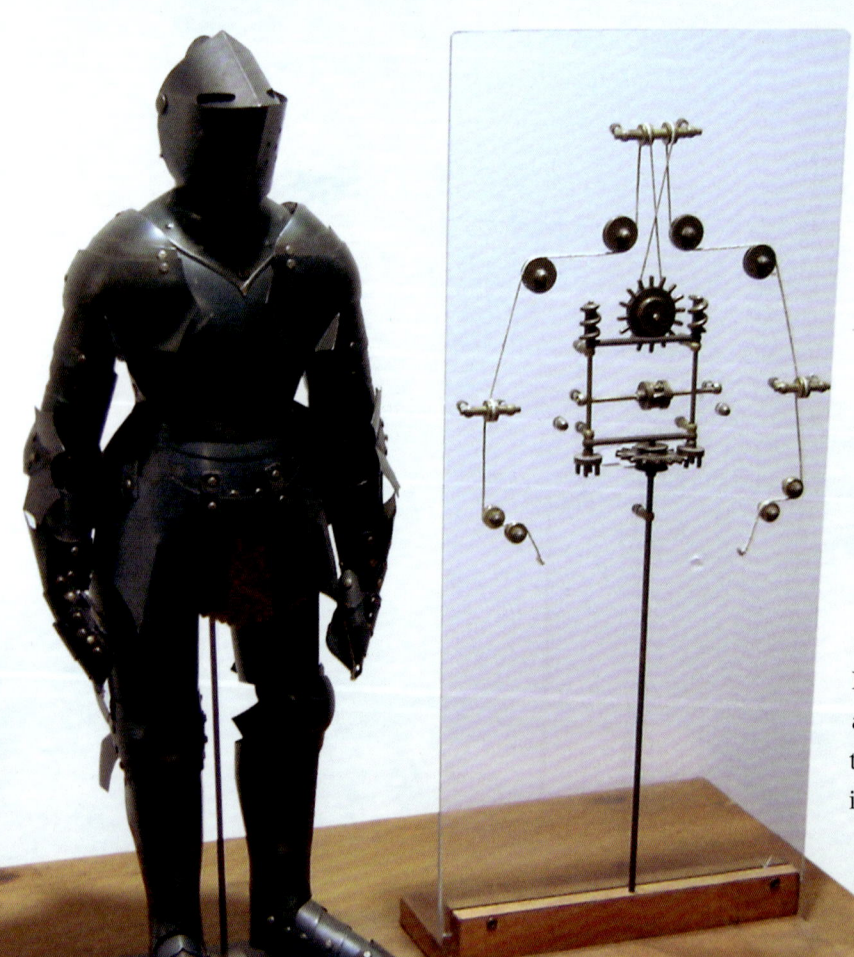

11 Punched Card Programs

CLOCKS AND CALCULATORS, EVEN SOME AUTOMATA, MAY COMPUTE THEIR OUTPUTS, but they are constrained to perform the same functions in the same way. What if a device could do anything given the right instructions?

Instructions to control equipment are now familiar to us as a program, and all true computers are programmable devices. The first programmable device was not a math machine at all, but a loom for weaving intricate textiles that was invented in the 1800s by Frenchman Joseph Jacquard. This was an age of mass production, and industrialists had embraced mechanical looms that could weave faster than people. These simple machines could produce unpatterned cloth with great efficiency, since every thread was from the same source. However, to add a pattern meant selecting individual threads, a fiddly business done by weavers using hooks. Jacquard invented a way of automating this system, making it faster and more accurate in the process—and requiring fewer workers.

He created a set of wooden cards punched with holes that determined which hooks could grab threads with each pass of the shuttle. History showed that Jacquard's innovation was not the loom itself but the method of encoding a particular controlling function on what became known as a punched card. Punched cards were also used to hold data and were being used as a means of programming computers into the 1950s.

Mill owners happily embraced Jacquard's invention, but loom operators saw their livelihoods threatened, and angry mobs smashed Jacquard looms.

12 The Analytical Engine

IN THE EARLY 1800S, THE TECHNOLOGY STILL HAD A LONG WAY TO GO to create a programmable clockwork computer, but it was the demand for complex math that drove it forward.

The Difference Engine was never fully built in Babbage's lifetime. It would have worked, but was just too expensive.

The turn of the 19th century was a time of great change. The Industrial Revolution, which had begun half a century before, was now in full swing in Britain, transforming the country into an economy built around the factory. The factory was centered around great engines that brought motive power unimaginable a generation before.

Alongside all this progress in industrialization, there were great leaps forward in scientific observation and discovery. With each new breakthrough, the mathematical burden on processing and analysis of data grew heavier. The English mathematician Charles Babbage became tired of all the errors that were inevitable when calculations were done by human hand. His solution was very much of its time. He devised a great engine that would do the math faster and with complete accuracy.

Making a difference

He released plans for his first device in the 1820s in the hope of raising money for its construction. This was the Difference Engine, a calculator that could handle 20-digit numbers—and it was not cheap. It would need 25,000 moving parts! All those components were there to perform simple additions and subtractions. Babbage's machine would use the "method of differences" where even complex functions are broken down into a long succession of simple sums. The process did need human input, but only in the form of setting the problem and turning a crank to drive the myriad cogs and gears. By 1832, Babbage had only got enough funding together to build about 15 percent of it. But this was just the beginning of Babbage's vision.

Going further

In 1839, Francois Michel-Marie Carquillat used a Jacquard loom, employing 24,000 cards, each with 1,000 hole positions, to weave a portrait in silk of Jacquard himself. Babbage had also been inspired by this system's power of precision in the design of his next device, the Analytical Engine. Undeterred by the expense of the Difference

Engine, this was a big step up. The Analytical Engine had even more parts, but that made it the first general-purpose programmable computer. And, just like a Jacquard loom, it was programmed using punched cards.

Old for new

The Analytical Engine was never built in full but partial replica versions have been created in museums. They look nothing like a modern computer, more like some steampunk musical instrument or food processor. The finished device would have filled a room—like any self-respecting engine—and its moving parts were meant to be turned by a steam engine! Nevertheless, the components that make up a modern computer were present in Babbage's design, albeit with much more Victorian-era names.

The Number Cards were concertinas of stiff paper marked with a code of holes punched in a pattern. These were fed into the engine and were used to input the numbers needed for the calculations—but could have carried any kind of input. The inputs were held in the Store, which was the Analytical Engine's memory or storage. The inputs in the Store were then called upon by what Babbage called the Mill, but in modern terms this was the CPU, or central processing unit. Babbage's Mill was controlled by the Operation Cards and the Variable Cards. These were two more sets of punched cards. The Operation Cards would now be termed the application. In Babbage's initial conception this would have been a complex mathematical function, but his device could have been applied in other ways. The variable cards worked as the addressing system, and so they controlled how numbers moved between the Store and the Mill—and back again. Finally, the engine's power supply was not a cable plugged into the wall, but a steam engine, which would have the power to turn the thousands of gears. In the end, Baggage's engines were little more than thought experiments— but what thoughts they were!

ARITHMOMETER

Babbage's designs were undoubtedly ingenious, but were preposterously overambitious for the time—even for now. Although he had secured government funding, Babbage's project was too costly and unwieldy. The plug was pulled in 1842. Less than a decade later, a more sober and less ambitious product came to market. This was the Arithmometer (below), the first mass-produced digital calculator. Frenchman Thomas de Colmar had spent 30 years getting it to market, and after Babbage's failure, the Arithmometer's advantages became ever more obvious. It was small, cheap, and above all sturdy enough to be transported across the world. It stayed in production until 1915!

13 Wired Telecoms

AN IMPORTANT PIECE OF THE PUZZLE OF COMPUTING is communications. Many of the ways we rely on computing today emerged from connecting them all together.

OPTICAL TELEGRAPH

The word "telegraph" comes from a visual messaging system from the 1790s. French brothers Claude and Ignace Chappe's "optical telegraph" consisted of pairs of movable arms that were positioned to represent different numbers and letters. The arms were mounted on towers spaced 3 to 6 miles (5 to 10 kilometers) apart. The brothers built a nationwide network with expert operators spelling out short messages that were repeated by the next tower in the chain. It took just 30 minutes for messages to travel 150 miles (240 km).

In 1830, Joseph Henry sent an electric current down a wire to activate an electromagnet 1 mile (1.5 kilometers) away, causing a bell to ring. British inventors William Cooke and Charles Wheatstone used this long-distance switch, or relay, in their electric telegraph system. This directed a current along a combination of wires that activated a needle to point to a specific letter or number. Soon, a much simpler system was introduced that did away with complex equipment to send and receive messages. It used Morse code, named for Samuel Morse, an American painter, and required only a spring-load switch to open and close the electric circuit. These on-off electric signals were received as combinations of buzzes, either short "dots" or long "dashes," which represented letters and numbers. This simple code whizzed along wires that were steadily rolled out across the world. In 1858, a new undersea cable meant it took an hour for messages to travel from Washington, D.C., to London, instead of ten days. The electromagnetic relay was at the heart of the telegraph, and as new telecoms technology took over in the 20th century, the relay would find a new role in the first digital computers.

A busy telegraph office in the 1890s uses printers that punch out messages as a code of holes. Operators could read this code more accurately than listening to transmitted tones.

14 Software

JUST AS CHARLES BABBAGE'S DREAM OF A MECHANICAL COMPUTER WAS BEING QUASHED, his young colleague was only just realizing its true potential. Her name was Ada Lovelace, the inventor of software.

Lovelace was unusual for a woman in 19th-century England in that she had been educated in math to a high level. She was a teenager when she met Babbage and first took an interest in his engines—as one of the few London socialites who understood it! She reportedly said that Babbage's devices would be able to weave numbers just as a Jacquard loom wove silk. In 1842, Babbage asked for her help in translating an essay about the Analytical Engine from French. She decided to add a few notes of her own. One of these, Note G, set out a method, or algorithm, for how the Analytical Engine could be programmed via punched cards to calculate Bernoulli numbers. These big numbers have many uses in mathematics and engineering, but in the 1840s took weeks to calculate by hand. Lovelace's program would have done it in minutes! The term "software" was only coined in 1958 to contrast it with the physical components of computer "hardware," but Lovelace's Note G is regarded as the first computer program.

Note G as it was published in Lovelace's English translation of Sketch of The Analytical Engine Invented by Charles Babbage *by Luigi Menabrea.*

Ada Lovelace, who Charles Babbage called "the Enchantress of Numbers," had big plans for developing the Analytical Engine to work with applications beyond pure math, such as music. She said that " … the Analytical Engine weaves algebraic patterns just as the Jacquard loom weaves flowers and leaves." Sadly, she died young in 1852.

15 Algorithms

THIS ANCIENT WORD HAS A NEW MEANING TODAY. We are dimly aware at least that "an algorithm" has some unseen control over our online lives. But what does that actually mean?

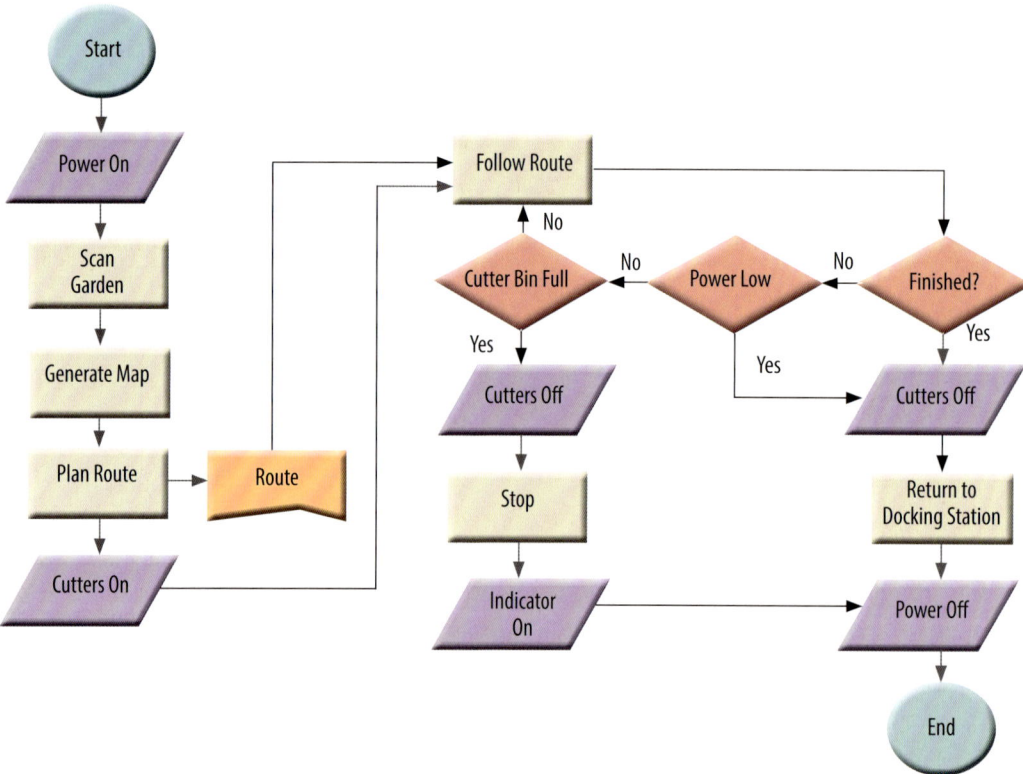

This flowchart shows the step-by-step control of a robotic lawn mower. The parallelograms indicate an input or output. The rectangles are a process, while the diamonds are a decision based on logic. How much of your life could be represented using these shapes and arrows?

The idea that an algorithm is the controlling force of a computer-based system is now familiar enough. That notion applies in exactly the same way to the settings on a washing machine as to the serving of personalized videos within a social media platform. In both cases the algorithm is simply a collection of instructions set out in a very particular order. Its purpose is to receive an input of data and then follow the steps rigorously to process it into an output, such as clean clothes or a video aimed at keeping your attention.

Before computers

The word algorithm has an interesting derivation. It comes from *Algoritmi*, the Latinized name of Muhammad ibn Musa al-Khwarizmi. A Persian mathematician from the 9th century CE, he is credited with inventing algebra, or at least giving it a name—it means something like "restoration of balance." Algebra is a technique that explores mathematical relationships where

This algorithm is used by every trader since the dawn of time. Buy low and sell high is the aim, but this set of instructions will confirm if you've succeeded.

The start of an 1854 book by George Boole, the mathematician who devised a new kind of math for converting the steps of an algorithm into simple (relatively) binary calculations. His system always gives one of two results: true or false.

An army of accountants in the days of pen and paper spent most of their time applying algorithms to data. The algorithms have not changed since, but office life certainly has.

numbers are replaced by placeholder symbols. Al-Khwarizmi created algebra to apply a formal procedure for solving quadratic equations, and Algoritmi's name came to be associated with this way of working. However, it was already very old. Although he did not use that term, Euclid himself had formulated an algorithm 2,300 years ago in his book *Elements*, history's first math textbook.

Control and reason

Ada Lovelace's first computer program in 1842, written for Charles Babbage's primitive computer (if it had been built) was an algorithm. Computer science was given a big boost a decade later with George Boole's book *An Investigation of the Laws of Thought*. He proposed algebra with just two values: 1 for *true* and 0 for *false*. Instead of addition, division, and the other operations of traditional algebra, Boolean operations were AND, OR, and NOT. Boolean calculations are perhaps disconcerting to the uninitiated. They only ever give an answer of 1 or 0, so 1 and 1 can equal 1, as can 0 and 0!

The purpose of Boole's new mathematics was to process logical functions. In terms that are perhaps familiar now, the operations will output either true or false when presented with particular starting conditions. When arrayed in a specific order, Boolean calculations offer a mathematical structure to algorithms, a structure that could be hardwired into computer processors.

16 Analog Computers

NATURE IS ANALOG, AND PERHAPS THIS IS WHY THE FIRST FUNCTIONING COMPUTERS WERE ALSO ANALOG. For most of its history, the story of computing has been in analog.

Older readers—those over about the age of 40—will attest that they were born into an analog world, but now find themselves in a digital one. The long-gone analog experience involved banging the TV set to make it work better—it often did the trick— and pressing the buttons on devices ever harder to make them respond. All of these techniques would not have been out of place on some analog computers.

We have already touched on analog computing devices, such as the Antikythera Mechanism and various kinds of mechanical clocks. Digital implies that a computer handles inputs and outputs, its programming, and storage all in terms of numbers, or digits. This can be interpreted as the components in a digital computer working in a "twofold" way, to paraphrase Francis Bacon. They are either on or off; inputs are either 1 or 0, true or false. However, digital computing also necessitates that everything is expressed as a number with a fixed and definite value. That includes things like the color of the sky and the sound of a voice just as much as the balance in a bank account or prices in an online store. An analog system does not deal in these fixed values. Instead, it responds to the continuous fluctuations in an input signal and creates outputs that fluctuate in harmony with them. While a digital system must be one thing or the other, the analog version can be anywhere in between.

In 1873, the Scottish scientist Lord Kelvin (he's better remembered for researching heat and energy) built this analog computer for calculating tide times anywhere in the world. Once set to a location, the interlinked wheels turned in concert to show the continuous ebb and flow of water. It was simple to maintain and proved accurate enough to stay in use until the 1970s.

FIRE CONTROL

In the early 1900s, the demand for computer power came from battleships. The crews of these monstrous ships lived or died on the accuracy of their immense guns, and targeting them required a lot of computation. Fire control systems—from the aiming director to the positioning of the gun's barrel—were carried out by an analog computer. The director device, once positioned by a lookout high up in the crow's nest, could send direction and distance inputs as electrical signals to a central electromechanical computer. These signals were used to calculate the angle and elevation of the guns, even taking into account the speed of the target and the flight time of the shells.

Going electric

Early analog computers got their computing power from—and were limited by—the size, shape, and interconnection of their gears and other moving parts. By the 20th century, the computers were receiving inputs as electrical signals. These signals conveyed information through fluctuations in current or voltage. This was also limited because there were upper and lower limits of these signals—too high and the computer literally exploded!

17 The Keyboard

FOR MUCH OF COMPUTING HISTORY, the primary input device has been the keyboard. Today's versions vary little from those used 150 years ago, but it took a few tries to get it right.

It is said that the computer is the most significant technological innovation since the printing press—and the keyboard is what links the two. The idea for a device that composed a page of written text using individually inked metal "type" is 500 years old. The first mass-produced version was the Hansen Writing Ball of 1870. The idea here was to spread the keys in an ergonomic way so they could be pressed down to type on a roll of paper underneath. The now familiar rectangular keyboard eventually took over. The keys were arranged so the more common letters were evenly spread between the typist's fingers. Legend has is that the sales team intervened to add an R to the top line of the English version so they could easily type out TYPEWRITER for clients.

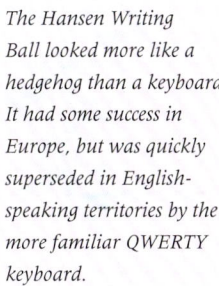

The Hansen Writing Ball looked more like a hedgehog than a keyboard. It had some success in Europe, but was quickly superseded in English-speaking territories by the more familiar QWERTY keyboard.

18 Voice Networks

THE TELEPHONE WAS A STEP UP FROM THE TELEGRAPH. It could transmit unique signals that encapsulated a sound, not mere tones. This technology is a direct link to the data networks that empower computing today.

The Internet and the World Wide Web were not even figments of the imagination back in the mid-19th century. However, they were both predicated on a technology that arose at this time: The telephone line. Even today, some computers will be talking to the world via a copper telephone wire, sending and receiving data encoded in sound—sound too high to hear, but sound nevertheless. This is all a far cry from the first sound of a voice sent along a wire back in 1861. The voice was of Philipp Reis, a German inventor who declared: "Das Pferd frisst keinen Gurkensalat." Or in English: "The horse does not eat cucumber salad." The reason this line (chosen because it contains a complexity of tones) is not well-known is because Reis's device was only one-way. A person (or horse) at the other end of the line could not respond.

The two-way telephone was perfected by the Scottish-Canadian Alexander Graham Bell. In fact, the American Elisha Gray is recorded as submitting a patent on the same day in 1876, but it was Bell who developed his system into a worldwide voice network, building one of the first technology companies to boot. (After all, it was the Bell Labs that created the world's first transistor in 1947 and changed the face of computing.)

Bell's system was an emulation of the animal ear. He researched this by talking into the ears of corpses to watch the ear drum vibrate. The physical sound wave in the air was turned into a like-for-like electrical signal. Bell's original device was upgraded by Thomas Edison's 1878 microphone, and phone lines began to be rolled out across the world. It took 100 years, but by the 1980s most buildings were connected—just as personal computers were beginning to be a feature of the home and workplace. What would happen next?

Alexander Graham Bell gives a demonstration of his telephone. He had had time to practice. His first phone conversation was reportedly to his assistant, saying, "Watson, come here, I want to see you." Bell had spilled acid, a component of his early microphone, all over the desk and needed some help clearing it up!

THE PHOTOPHONE

Alexander Graham Bell was a great innovator, and he imagined a telephone that connected people without the need for wires. The result was the photophone, the world's first wireless telephone system. Words spoken into a tube made a mirror vibrate, changing the amount of sunlight reflected back to a receiving mirror, where light waves were converted back to sound. There were practical problems—it didn't work on cloudy days—and it was never used widely. However, it was a forerunner of the fiber optics now used to transmit telephone and Internet signals at the speed of light.

19 Holleriths's Tabulator

A STRENGTH OF COMPUTING, COMMONLY RECOGNIZED TODAY, is the superhuman scale of its abilities. This power was illustrated first by a machine built to record those most human traits of birth, death, and taxes.

BIG BLUE BEGINS

Hollerith was an inventor and academic, and not best suited for business. After the success of his machines in government, he had trouble finding new markets. New partners joined his Tabulating Machine Company and merged it with a series of competitors. The bigger market was in cash registers and specialist calculating machines. In 1914, Thomas Watson, a New York accountant, joined the company and became a new driving force. He streamlined the complex corporate structure and doubled revenues within four years. In 1924, Watson and Hollerith's company was renamed the International Business Machines Corporation, soon to be much better known as IBM. Nicknamed "Big Blue," IBM was to become the first computer giant, producing the world's biggest and fastest computers well past the dawn of the personal-computing age.

The United States Constitution makes clear that every ten years a census is required to ensure that every citizen is paying a fair share of their taxes. A century or so after Independence, and following the Emancipation of 1863, this task was getting out of hand. Millions of pieces of paper had to be grouped for taxation and election purposes, which meant they were all read, counted, and sorted by hand, using pen and paper. The 1880 U.S. census took most of the following decade to process. The population was booming, and if nothing was done the 1890 census would not be completed before the 1900 count! In 1889, an American engineer named Herman Hollerith answered the call for help with a mechanical computer.

Hollerith was inspired by watching bus conductors punch holes at different parts of a ticket to indicate what journey passengers were making. He devised a way of creating a census data record of every U.S. citizen—their age, state, etc—as a card with a set of holes punched in it. Hollerith's Tabulator sorted the records automatically, and more quickly than a human. Nevertheless, a person was needed to operate the machine.

Electrical power

While using the legacy tech of punched cards from Jacquard looms and Babbage's engines, Hollerith also embraced the new by including electricity. The card reader had a bath of mercury beneath it. Pins were lowered from above, and any that corresponded with a hole dropped through to the mercury and completed an electrical circuit. In this way the data of each card became a set of on–off signals that could be sorted according to the tabulator's program.

The wooden handle of the card reader is seen on the tabulator's desktop—a literal one in this case. The dials on the tabulator kept records of the count as it proceeded. The cabinet to the right contained filing boxes. When a card had been read, the correct box would open so the operator could slot that card into it.

20 Human Computers

WHILE MECHANICAL COMPUTERS WERE SHOWING THEIR WORTH AT THE START OF THE 20TH CENTURY, for decades to come the term "computer" would still mean a human worker.

Very special people appear occasionally with seemingly supernatural calculating abilities. This ability is called savantism, and one famous mathematical savant was Jedediah Buxton, who lived in England in the 18th century. It is said that Buxton could not read or write and had limited general knowledge. He had no formal math lessons but he used numbers to describe whatever he saw. He is said to have measured the area of a country estate simply by walking over it, and coming up with an answer in square inches!

People with obvious mathematical abilities could find work as computers. Their job was to focus on the long and arduous calculations that were written out on paper—and then checked and rechecked. This was very much a backroom role, and so it was more open to women, who were barred from more public-facing jobs in science. A famous team of computers was put together at the observatory of Harvard University. All women, they included Annie Jump Cannon, who set up the system for classifying stars that is largely followed today (with some additions), and Henrietta Swan Leavitt, who discovered a way to measure the distances between stars. Her work was used by Edwin Hubble to discover the Universe is expanding. Even in the early days of NASA the computers were women, not machines. They included the now famous "hidden figures" like Katherine Johnson and Dorothy Vaughan. The calculations of these African American women were crucial to the success of the space program.

Katherine Johnson, a computer at NASA, calculated the flight paths of the spacecraft that took the first Americans into space.

21 Wireless Communication

RADIO IS AN UNSEEN LINCHPIN IN MODERN COMPUTING. Through Wi-Fi, Bluetooth, and cellular networks, it keeps your devices connected as you roam free.

The wireless world exists thanks to an invisible electromagnetic wave discovered by the German physicist Heinrich Hertz in 1887. Hertz could not see a use for his radio waves, but others could, including Nikola Tesla, the Serbian engineer who had been instrumental in creating the electrical power grid. He imagined a communication system where radio pulses were transmitted through Earth's interior. It never succeeded. In 1899, the Italian Guglielmo Marconi sent a Morse code signal from England to France, and two years later across the Atlantic. In order to transmit complex signals, such as the sound of a voice (or encoded computer data), the radio transmitter needed a high-frequency electrical current to provide a fluctuating radio wave. Such a device, an alternator, was used by the Canadian Reginald Fessenden to broadcast the first voices and music by radio in 1906.

Guglielmo Marconi with a wireless telegraph set. Equipment like this found a market in ship communications. The RMS Titanic used it to raise the alarm with the recently adopted SOS Morse signal—but too late for many, of course.

22 Thermionic Valve

DIGITAL COMPUTING REQUIRES A TWO-STATE DEVICE, that operates according to a binary, on–off, code. Such an item arose from a light-bulb moment.

This example of a thermionic valve looks very similar to its parent technology, the light bulb. The most obvious difference is that the spiralled filament that emits light and heat is surrounded by a metal plate collecting the current created by the Edison effect.

In 1904, British scientist John Ambrose Fleming made one of the most important breakthroughs in electronics. It used the Edison effect, discovered by the famous American inventor who had created one of the earliest light bulbs. The effect is a flow of electrons from the hot filament of an incandescent bulb to another electrode. Fleming used this to boost a weak radio signal by wiring a vacuum tube (early light bulbs used vacuums) into a radio-receiving circuit. The radio signal created an electric current which was replicated by the effect, only this second current was more powerful and thus created a louder sound. This invention was named the Fleming valve. It was "thermionic" because its action was thermal, or linked to heat. The valve was the forerunner of the diodes and triodes that were used in the first electronic computers. By applying a current to the extra electrode, the valve could be used as a switch, turning a current on or off at great speed and in large numbers.

23 Robots

THE DREAM OF AUTONOMOUS MACHINES THAT DO ALL THE WORK FOR US IS ONE THAT, ONCE GLIMPSED, IS IMPOSSIBLE TO FORGET. Today we call these machines robots. They are a very real part of modern technology, thanks to improvements in motors and materials. And the computer-controlled intelligence that would make these machines even more useful to us seems nearer than ever, too.

It is perhaps only recently that robots have emerged as science fact rather than science fiction. The public conception of the intelligent robot is still as a character in a futuristic alternative world. The term "robot" originated in a work of fiction, coined by Karel Capek, a Czech playwright. His 1920s play, *R.U.R.*, was about artificial men built to serve humans. *Robota* is a Slavic word for menial work, and that seemed to suit. The play is a satire about how technology can brutalize a society as much as it can free us from hardship. Spoiler alert: The play's robots rise up and kill all humans. The end.

A curious human shakes hands with the British-made Eric the Robot on its visit to the United States in 1929.

Electric humans

Capek's play caught the global imagination. His robots were flesh and blood, perhaps grown rather than built (it is not made clear), but when it came to building real-world robots, they were invariably metal, more Tin Man from *The Wizard of Oz* than the *Terminator*. In 1928, British engineers revealed Eric. Eric could stand up, sit down, and speak (a hidden operator's voice was received by radio—as a display of a Marconi product.) In 1938, Westinghouse made Elektro, who could walk, listen to commands, and reply with recorded messages. The 8-ft (2-m) machine also had a pet robot dog, Sparko.

THE THREE LAWS OF ROBOTICS

Isaac Asimov, another author that wrote stories about robotics, set out three rules that would put the balance of power in our favor and ensure intelligent robots would serve, rather than destroy humanity.

Asimov's three laws:
1 A robot may not injure a human being or, through inaction, allow a human being to come to harm.
2 A robot must obey the orders given it by human beings, except where such orders would conflict with the First Law.
3 A robot must protect its own existence, as long as such protection does not conflict with the First or Second Laws.

Worker power

In 1961, a real-life robot was put into production. This was Unimate, the grandfather of today's factory robots. It was a simple robot arm with six joints that moved independently. This is known as six degrees of freedom. The arm was preset to carry out the same maneuvers over and over again. It never got tired or bored and was able to do dangerous jobs, such as die casting, where human workers would be exposed to poisonous fumes.

The successors of Unimate can be programmed to carry out a range of movements. Mostly, this is done by simply moving the arm by hand in the correct sequence. The robot remembers each step and will repeat them exactly. The motors that move each joint are called effectors, because they act to change the robot in some way. The business end of a robot is the end effector. In Unimate's case this was a pincer, but factory bots hold wrenches, spray guns, or welding torches.

As well as effectors, every robot has sensors and a processor. The sensors in a robot arm will track the motion of each joint, keeping a record of the direction and extent of its movement. The processor, which is essentially a computer either inside the robot or connected to it, uses these sensory inputs to maintain a record of the robot's overall position: All it needs do is move to the next step in the pre-learned sequence. A smarter system includes feedback loops whereby the processor is kept updated with information, such as an unexpected obstacle or blockage. Only one thing for it. Stop!

R.U.R., *or Rossum's Universal Robots, was performed across the world to rave reviews.*

ELMER AND ELSIE

In the late 1940s, a neurophysiologist called William Gray Walter created a very different kind of robot. They were simple wheeled machines with a protective cover, and would be called turtle robots today. Walter called them Elmer and Elsie. They were the world's first autonomous robots. Walter gave them a light and a touch sensor, each wired to a separate motor. He found that even this basic setup was enough for the turtles to find their way around obstacles and locate an illuminated charging station. The robots' simple actions could have been interpreted as reason and even emotion. Walter is hailed as a founding figure in AI and cybernetics.

24 Display Screens

From desktops to phones and smart televisions, the display (or screen) has always been the primary output device of the personal computer age. This was helped in no small part by every home already having a TV.

FLAT SCREENS

A nickname for the TV is the tube, because the original sets were long vacuum tubes. Today's flat displays are layers of LEDs (light-emitting diodes) and liquid crystals. The LEDs produce light that passes through layers of liquid crystal divided into pixels. Each pixel blocks or transmits the light, depending on whether it is electrified or not. To create color, the pixels are subdivided into red, green, and blue filters. The pattern of sub-pixels, refreshed many times a second, creates the images we see.

The first TV picture was of a hand puppet called "Stooky Bill." The puppet was operated by John Logie Baird, the inventor of the television. William Edward Taynton, who just happened to be working in Baird's neighboring office, was sat in front of the screen and became the first person to watch television. The date was October 2, 1925.

A display screen relies on the "persistence of vision" where our brains create smoothly moving images from a rapid flicker of static images. A television captures still images of a moving subject dozens of times a second, and transmits them in the right order to be recreated on a distant display. These images are recreated faster than a blinking eye by sweeping a flickering "cathode ray" (a beam of electrons) inside a glass screen. The inner coating glows under the beam, tracing out an image. Television broadcasts began in the late 1920s, but the TV revolution really rolled out in the 1950s as sets became cheaper. The same cathode-ray tube devices were used in "terminals" for huge mainframe computers, and in the 1970s and '80s tech enthusiasts were wiring their TVs to their primitive personal computers. The computing revolution was going to happen on TV.

John Logie Baird sits in his original television studio. His first machine used mechanical means to capture an electrical "shadow" of the scene. A smoother all-electric version soon replaced this original.

25 Vannevar Bush

BUSH WAS THE CHIEF SCIENCE ADVISOR TO THE WHITE HOUSE during World War II, and so is most associated with setting up the Manhattan Project. However, his early work in computing has proved prescient.

Vannevar Bush was an electrical engineer in the days when that was an exciting field at the cutting edge of technology, akin to the Silicon Valley tech culture of today. He went to work at General Electric and then moved to further his studies at MIT (Massachusetts Institute of Technology). After spells teaching elsewhere, he ended up back there on the faculty, eventually turning his attention to developing a differential analyzer. This was an analog computer that could solve differential equations by integration. To do this aspect of calculus by hand is long-winded, to say the least, but a mechanism geared in the correct ratios could be a physical representation of the real-life variables, and thus output results. Lord Kelvin's tide-predicting machine was a kind of differential analyzer. Along with his colleague Harold Hazen, Bush (who later said he had been unaware of Kelvin's device at the time) created a more versatile version. It was able to amplify the results to create a more precise figure.

Four electromechanical differential analyzers at Cambridge University. In the 1930s, these were the supercomputers of their day.

As well as being a practical person, Bush was also at the forefront of the theory of digital computing. He taught Boolean algebra to electrical engineers and one of his students, Claude Shannon, would later join Bush and Hazen to create digital circuitry. Bush also recognized the great potential of information machines. With such a device, he said, "A library of a million volumes could be compressed into one end of a desk." He was talking about Memex, his theoretical system for storing and linking text—a "memory extension." Memex users would store their personal library on microfilm. Each library entry would be associated, or linked, with others that contained further information. Bush's vision of the future needed a few more decades to reach the mainstream, but his idea of intuitive connections was an influence on the "hyperlink" in the first website of 1991. Hyperlinks became a foundational feature of the World Wide Web, so, just as Bush predicted, everything we need is just a click away.

26 The Turing Machine

THE FIRST DIGITAL COMPUTER WAS NEVER INTENDED TO BE BUILT. It was just a thought experiment, a virtual device that could solve a leading math problem of the day. Only later was its true potential recognized.

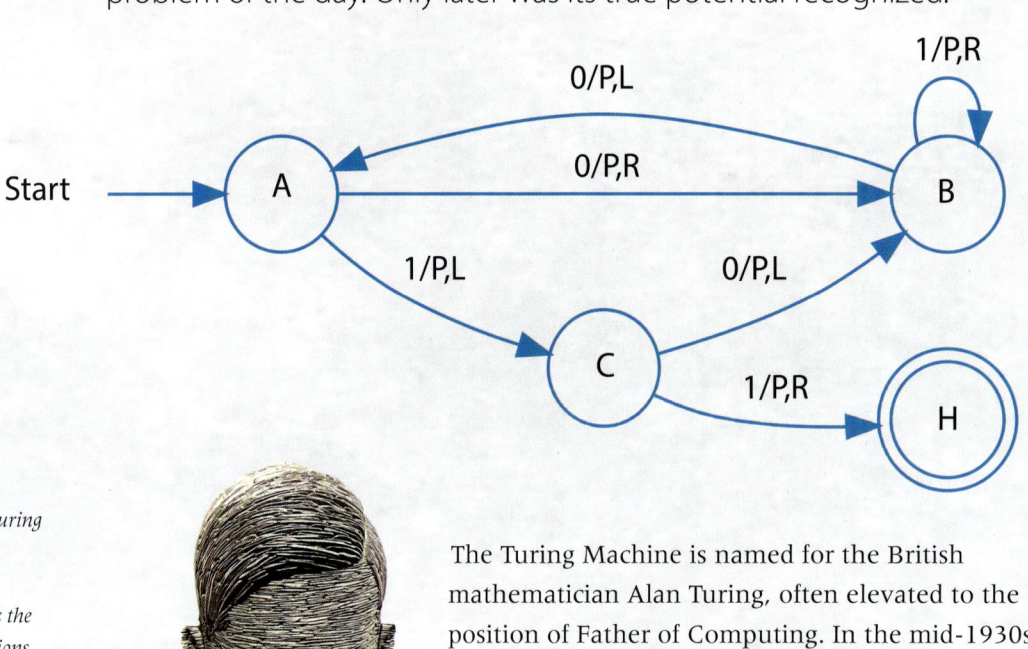

This flowchart shows the possible changes in "state" of the Turing machine—in other words what it is doing now and what it will do next, if anything. Will it reach H for halt? Or will it just go around and around in a loop?

A statue of Alan Turing stands at Bletchley Park in southern England. This was the secret communications headquarters that cracked the enemy codes in World War II. Turing made a major contribution to that effort.

The Turing Machine is named for the British mathematician Alan Turing, often elevated to the position of Father of Computing. In the mid-1930s, math was in a bit of a crisis. Attempts to formalize the whole endeavor had done just the opposite. Gödel's Incompleteness Theorem (see box) suggested that math was no longer the ultimate source of truth it seemed, and had a flaw that might mean it had reached its limits of usefulness. Against this backdrop, Turing became interested in the *Entscheidungsproblem*, or "decision problem," posed by the German mathematician David Hilbert in 1928. Hilbert wondered if it was possible to use a set of rules to ascertain whether a piece of mathematical logic, a kind of algorithm essentially, would create a result. If it didn't, the logical steps would iterate forever and never reach a conclusion. Telling the former type from

INCOMPLETENESS

Turing's work was in part inspired by Kurt Gödel's Incompleteness Theorems. The Austrian's 1931 paper illustrated that all mathematics is incomplete. It says that a consistent system has no statements that can be proven both true and false, but it must also contain statements that cannot be proved or disproved. Secondly, no such system can be proved to be consistent within itself. This changed math—and helped create computer science!

the latter would not only save a lot of time, but also unlock a further piece of the math puzzle. Hilbert and others created a language for these algorithms, but then Gödel shook the mathematical world to a stop.

Reaching a decision

In 1937 Turing, then working at King's College, Cambridge, published a paper that said there could never be a universal mechanism for identifying which algorithms concluded and which did not. The only way to find out for sure is to run the algorithm. Turing's proof involved a "virtual machine" that could indeed run any algorithm. The clever part was that it was all in his head.

The Turing machine had two main parts. First there was a tape, infinite in length if necessary. The tape was divided along its length into zones of equal size. The zones each contained a coded symbol. The simplest option was a binary code of 1s and 0s, but Turing was not interested in the code itself. The machine knew the correct code and could read everything perfectly. The second part was the reader, which could move along the tape from zone to zone. (It might be more practical to move the tape, but the function is the same.) Having read the data in a zone, the reader inputted it into a set of instructions—the algorithm—to find what to do next: The reader could move to the next zone, back to the one before, or stay where it was. It could also rewrite the data in that zone, and re-input it. If the algorithm reached a conclusion, the Turing machine halted. If it did not, then it would run forever.

Entering the real world

Quite how Turing used this machine to negate the Decision Problem involves another level of complexity. He strung machines together in series to create a logical paradox that sealed the deal. Let's just say he was a clever guy! Turing made an initial world-changing step when he realized that an algorithm could be encoded on the tape. So, the machine could be used to run any computable algorithm, the kind of work being carried out at the time by human computers or differential analyzers.

Turing's thought experiment caught the attention of other scientists, and, in 1938, Turing traveled to the United States to meet the other "father of computing," John von Neumann. The pair discussed how his virtual machine might be made into a real device. After World War II, von Neumann developed an architecture of relays that made it possible to put a version of the Turing Machine into action: The first electronic digital computers were born.

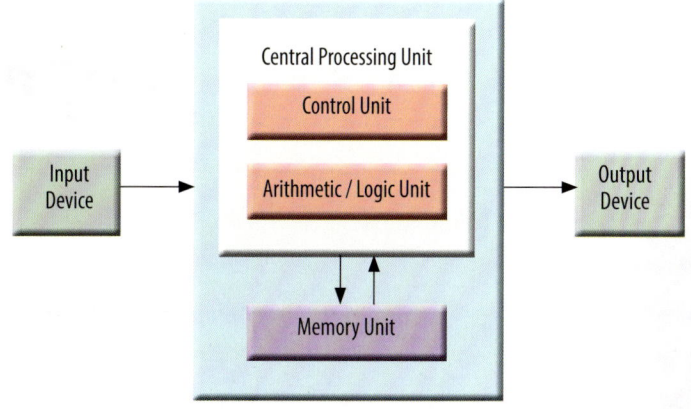

The basic setup of a computer was created by John von Neumann when he constructed a physical Turing machine. The setup is known today as the "von Neumann architecture."

27 Using Logic

The stage was now set for the digital computer. On one side was the mathematics of logic and on the other, the fast-switch technology of valves and relays. The question was, could they be made to work together?

The first actor to take center stage was Konrad Zuse, a young German engineer who could not wait for the technology to catch up with his ambition. He wanted to build a computer that could process Boole's algebra using a series of on-off switches. This had been suggested way back in 1886 by the American logician Charles Sanders Peirce, who proposed using electromagnetic relays like those in a telegraph system.

Zuze was a remarkable autodidact and built his first device, the Z1, at home in 1938. The Z1 was a programmable calculator. Z2 was an updated version fitted with telephone relays. Zuse had big plans for Z3 and had initially thought of using valves. However, they were expensive to produce and in short supply in Nazi Germany, which was busy re-arming the country. He was nevertheless part-sponsored by the Aerodynamic Research Institute, who thought Z3 would help develop faster aircraft and rockets. So Zuse built it using relays, and as a result it was slow and prone to failure—and in the end impractical. Despite its limitations, Zuse had created an electromechanical digital computer using designs and concepts that were similar to, but arrived at entirely independently of, the likes of Turing, von Neumann, and Claude Shannon.

Switching circuits

Shannon was an electrical engineering student of Vannevar Bush at MIT, and in the late 1930s, he developed switching circuits that used Boolean equations to control when some or all of the circuit was switched on or off. A Boolean equation deals with

In 1950, Shannon built a mechanical mouse called Theseus that was controlled by logic circuits. Theseus was autonomous and was sent around a maze with a unit area of 25. Each unit had adjustable walls, so the maze was different each time. Theseus found its way to a target by trial and error, but stored a map of the maze built up during its travels. If placed anywhere it had been before, it could find its way to the target again without any errors.

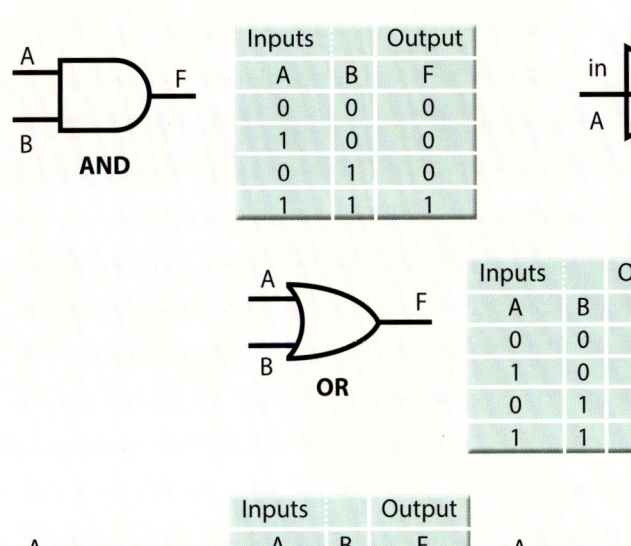

Logic gates are built from Boolean operations. AND, NOT, and OR are single operations. NOT only requires a single input, but others require two (at least). Other gates are composites of several operations. For example, NAND is NOT and AND working together.

true–false problems of different kinds. Shannon's circuits became known as logic gates. Each one indicated true or false, 1 or 0, by turning the current on or off. These circuits are the foundation of digital computing. A logic gate can be made in many ways—perhaps even mechanically by toppling dominoes or rolling balls—and today they are nanoscale objects etched with meticulous precision on microchips. However, Shannon would have been thinking more of thermionic valves and large circuitry wired up by hand.

A particular kind of valve, the triode, was most suited to the job of a logic gate. A triode can work as a switch, and several wired together can convert inputs, be they a 1 (current on) or 0 (current off), into an output of 1 or 0 based on the relevant Boolean operations. For example, an AND gate always outputs 0 unless both inputs are 1. This follows the logic of a light bulb (the output) that only turns on if both light switches (the input) are switched on at the same time.

MINIVAC AND BEYOND

Shannon was an early bloomer and made his mark on computer science—and the history of the world—early in his career. He had many other interests, as he worked at MIT until the 1970s and stayed long after he was supposed to be retired. In 1961 he launched the Minivac (below), thought by some to be the first personal computer. You couldn't play games on it or write documents, though. It was intended as a teaching tool or educational toy that could be used as a practical guide to the workings and behaviors of digital circuits. Users wired together the components in different setups and could input numbers by turning the dial. The dial turned by itself to give the outputs. Shannon also invented a device for predicting the odds in roulette. This pocket-sized machine is said to be the first wearable computer!

28 Enigma Code

WHEN WORLD WAR II BEGAN, GERMAN FORCES HAD THE UPPER HAND with their communications. They used Enigma machines to hide messages in an uncrackable code—or at least that is what they thought.

The Enigma machine was easy to use—every user had to follow the same setup—yet it produced a dazzlingly complex cipher. Anyone who wanted to crack a message would have to try 158,962,555,217,826,360,000 possible keys to decipher it. As it happened, by the end of World War II, the Allies had secretly been able to do just that. They had succeeded thanks to a lot of resources and technological innovation, but also thanks to mathematicians. The most famous of those was Alan Turing, who devised primitive electromechanical computers to get the job done.

The machine
The Enigma machine had a keyboard and a panel of 26 letters that could light up. Inside were three rotors marked with numbers. They were each mounted on a spindle and set to one of 26 possible positions. The keyboard connected to the rotors via convoluted wires that could be rearranged by moving the plugs around. On any given day, every Enigma machine was set up in the same way, with the rotors and plugs in the same starting positions. The rotors could be swapped around to further obfuscate the code.

The operator typed a message on the keyboard, and each letter resulted in another letter lighting up on the panel. The receiving operator needed to just type the lit-up letters into another machine. The original "plaintext" was then spelled out in lights on the panel. The next day, with a new rotor and plug setup, the same message would be encoded differently.

Cracking the code
The operators of the Enigma machines disseminated the rotor and plug positions in the first message each morning. If this could be cracked, then eavesdroppers could use their own machines to decipher any message. Poland's Cipher

The electromechanical Enigma machine looked every bit a Nazi typewriter. A press of a key lit up a corresponding light of a different—in fact any—letter. The machines were captured by Allied Forces, and, steadily, the codebreakers got to work.

Bureau had the first go. Marian Rejewski proved to be their star man. He found he could use the last few letters in the morning messages to narrow down the rotor settings to 100,000 options from trillions! Rejewski built a device, codenamed the Bomba, to simulate all the possible rotor positions. The Bomba cracked the code in under 24 hours.

Ever cautious, the Germans enhanced Enigma's security in 1938 by adding more rotors and plugs, which pushed the possible setups into the quintillions! This was when English mathematician Alan Turing joined the effort. German units transmitted the weather at 6 p.m., and this message would surely contain the word "weather." Working at Bletchley Park, Turing built his own Bombe that took five hours to check every permutation possible, with any rotor setting, for weather words. If a word such as "weather" came up, then that permutation was checked with a real Enigma machine. It was not always completely correct first time, but the errors helped indicate the actual settings that were needed. Eventually, a day's code was cracked, allowing all other messages to be decoded. The Bombe was electromechanical, and by 1943 it had been upgraded with a new machine that used thermionic valves. This was Colossus, the creation of Tommy Flowers (not Turing), and it was the world's first electronic digital computer. More on that soon.

The Bombe at Bletchley Park, the Allied codebreaking HQ in England. It was devised by Alan Turing to try out every possible combination of an extract of code. The process had to start afresh each day.

SIGNALS INTELLIGENCE

Since the days of the telegraph, the value of monitoring telecommunications has been recognized by the spooks and spies of the great powers. The codebreakers at Bletchley Park were part of GCHQ (Government Communications Headquarters), a UK intelligence service that was set up during World War I. GCHQ's experience showed the power of computing in the analysis and deciphering of enemy communications. The wartime US equivalent (above) was based in Virginia, and is now part of the NSA (National Security Agency). No one is telling, but it is probable that the NSA, GCHQ, and other spy agencies have some of the largest and fastest computers in the world.

29 The First Network

COMPUTER SCIENCE IS AS MUCH ABOUT communication as calculation, and that all began with a typewriter and telephone line.

MODEM
An abbreviated portmanteau of "modulator–demodulator," this device translated data into a telephone signal—and then back again. Once a ubiquitous (and noisy) object, its function is now handled by routers.

In 1940, George Stibitz was working at Bell Labs, the research hub of a telecoms company originally set up by Alexander Bell, the inventor of the telephone. Stibitz had created the Complex Number Calculator (CNC), a precursor of the digital computer, a few years before. The CNC was located in New York City, and when Stibitz was at a mathematics conference at Dartmouth College in New Hampshire, he wanted to demonstrate its abilities. He did not need to bring the device with him. Instead, he connected to it by telephone, using a teleprinter to send commands and receive the results. This demonstration of remote working was an early glimpse at what would be possible with computer networks and cloud computing.

Teleprinters had a keyboard and sent text as a binary code of on–off signals.

30 Colossus: The First of Billions

WITH SEVERAL PREDECESSORS, AND BILLIONS OF DEVICES TO FOLLOW, this computer from 1943 marked a turning point.

Communications in the Enigma code were generally between the German military command and field units. The strategic communication of the Nazis' High Command was encrypted using a different coding system, called Lorenz. Cracking the Lorenz code used a similar technique as the one deployed by the Bombe, but was carried out by a different machine: Colossus. Alan Turing contributed to the programming of Colossus, but the device was constructed by Tommy Flowers, a telephone engineer. He used 4,000 valves to build the CPU. Coded text was inputed on punched paper tape and the decoded plaintext was printed out by a typewriter. As such, Colossus was the first electronic digital computer that could be programmed. However, unlike later computing devices, Colossus had no memory and it was reprogrammed by rewiring components.

31 ENIAC: The Giant Electronic Brain

As wartime secrecy fell away, computing became a public topic. The first device to capture the popular imagination was the Electronic Numerical Integrator and Computer—better known as the "Giant Brain."

The year 1946 saw another of many firsts in digital computing. This one was ENIAC, as the Electronic Numerical Integrator and Computer was better known. This was the world's first general-purpose, digital, electronic computer. ENIAC was a step on from Colossus, because it was programmable without needing to be disassembled. This meant it could be turned to any task once programmed via a plugboard that allowed technicians to reconfigure the connections between its 17,000 valves and nearly 100,000 other components. Despite this advance, ENIAC took days—if not weeks—to program.

ENIAC did a number of tasks, including calculations for weather forecasts and crunching data for the military. It could perform 385 multiplications, 40 divisions, or three square-root calculations per second. Like the Analytical Engine (and Colossus), ENIAC was able to use conditional branching in its programs. This meant it could alter the order of execution of instructions based on the value of data. For example, its algorithm could say: "If Y is greater than 10, then go to line 26, else go to line 25."

ENIAC filled a basement at the University of Pennsylvania. It had 40 8-ft- (2.4 m) tall panels arranged around three walls.

MERCURY DELAY LINE

This was an early data storage system. Electrical pulses of data were converted into sound and sent as slow waves through tubes of mercury. The ripples were reconverted to electricity at each end, and re-emitted as sound. Stored data bounced around inside the tube until it was retrieved by the computer. One line held 576 bits, or the code for 32 letters.

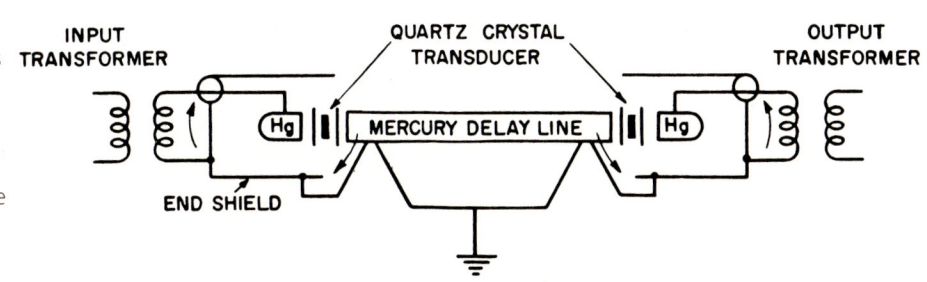

32 Finding Bugs

COMPUTING IS A FIDDLY BUSINESS. LITERALLY BILLIONS OF THINGS CAN GO WRONG. Errors in software and flaws in hardware are known as bugs. The first bug was identified in 1947—and was an actual moth!

MILLENNIUM BUG

The most famous bug of all was the Millennium Bug, a feature of how dates were recorded. Prior to the 21st century, years were given two digits, and so without changes the year 2000 would be recorded as 00 and be confused with 1900! A vast upgrade was made to critical systems and the "bug" had no ill effects.

The bug was recorded by researchers at Harvard University. Their computer, the Harvard Mark II, was not behaving as expected, outputting obvious errors. They opened up the computer and found a moth flapping around inside, disrupting the connections. The Mark III was funded by the U.S. Navy, who wanted it to calculate ballistic data for developing missiles (and space rockets). Legend has it that Grace Hopper, a Naval representative on the Harvard team, named computer bugs after this literal bug. Hopper went on to be an important figure in developing software languages, such as COBOL. (While this is the first computer bug, Thomas Edison, the inventor *extraordinaire*, often referred to glitches in his designs as "bugs.")

The term has persisted and grown. Error checks of software are known as debugging. Programmers will generally use debuggers for this. A debugger is a type of software that detects where in the code an error occurs.

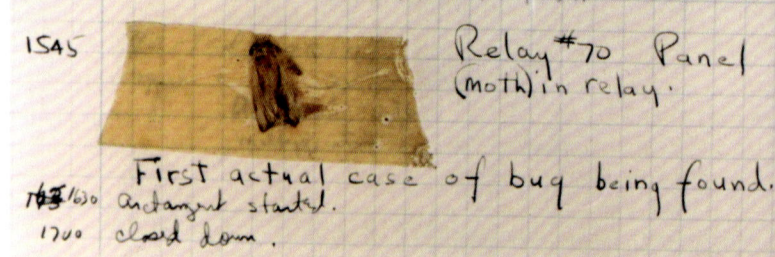

The world's first computer bug is taped to the log of the Harvard Mark II computer.

33 The Transistor

WITH THE THEORY IN PLACE, THE COMPUTING AGE needed some innovation to reach its full promise. That arrived in 1947 with the invention of semiconductors, which delivered more than hoped for!

A digital computer's circuitry needs to perform Boolean operations, and it does those using logic gates (see page 39). The circuitry needs to represent only binary values of 1 and 0 for it to do this job, and it does that with the most simple of electrical components: The switch. An open switch breaks the circuit, stops the flow of current and represents a 0. A closed switch allows current to flow and represents a 1. Of course, the whole point of a computer is that these switches open and close automatically, and so require a more advanced kind of switch. The first candidate was the electromagnetic relay, a switching device that was itself controlled by an electrical current. They had been perfected for use in telegraph and telephone networks. The Z3 computer used them, but relays are slow and cumbersome, and impractical for the purposes of computing. A thermionic triode could switch on and off much faster, and early digital computers from Colossus and ENIAC on were based on them. But thousands of valves were needed, filling entire rooms—and frequently burning out.

Semiconductors

By the 1930s, a completely new kind of switch had been theorized, called a field effect transconductance varistor, or transistor for short. This imagined device would be a semiconductor, a material that could switch from being an insulator that blocked current, to one that conducted it—and then switch back. It was ideal for computer circuitry.

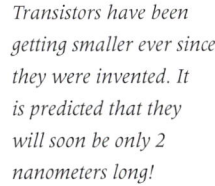

> **RADAR**
>
> Germanium-based semiconductors had their genesis in radar. This long-range sensing technology—used as a decisive weapon in World War II—relied on ultra-pure germanium crystals. These were used to amplify the faint echoes of radio waves that were bouncing back from distant objects beyond the horizon. Silicon crystals were also used in radar technology, and their semiconducting properties saw them eventually supersede germanium as the main material for making transistors.

In 1947, a trio of researchers working at Bell Labs, John Bardeen, Walter Brattain, and their supervisor, William Shockley, succeeded in building such a device. It was made from germanium and gold, and had three electrical contacts—the source, gate, and drain. This allowed it to perform the same function as a triode valve. The flow of electricity from the source to the drain could be switched on and off by applying an electric current to the gate. The transistor was better than the triode valve because it was smaller and compact—and would get much smaller in later decades—and it could be relied on to switch on and off thousands of times a second. Computing was about to be revolutionized.

Transistors have been getting smaller ever since they were invented. It is predicted that they will soon be only 2 nanometers long!

HOW IT WORKS

Transistors use semiconducting material to make a sandwich. 1) The "bread" is n-type material that has been "doped," so it contains more electrons than normal. The filling is a p-type semiconductor that has fewer electrons, so more spaces, or "holes," where electrons might fit. 2) At the interface, electrons leak from the n-type to the p-type, creating a "depletion zone." There is no way for a current to flow through the transistor, and so it is switched "off." 3) When a charge is added to the p-type layer, the electrons are pulled toward it. 4) This creates a bridge of charge between the n-type layers, and a current flows. The transistor is now "on."

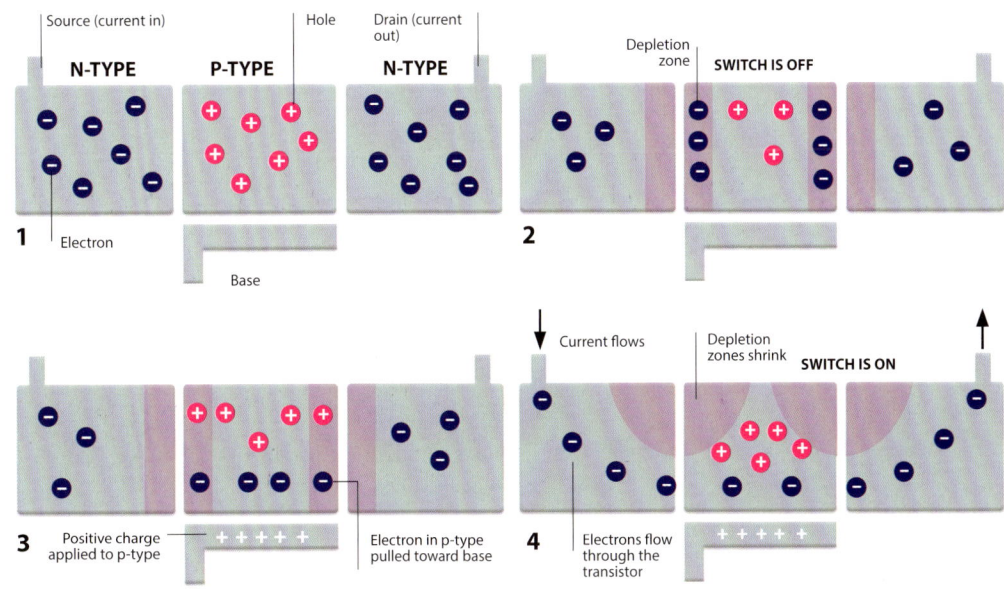

34 Information Theory

As computer processors became more advanced, computer scientists found that they were not really working with electricity or even digits. Instead, a computer holds information.

The fleeting electrical currents shimmering through a computer processor are a physical manifestation of information. The founding figure of logical circuits, Claude Shannon, also created information theory, which measures the storage and transmission of information. We have Shannon to thank for the word "bit" as a contraction of "binary digit." A single bit measures a 0 or 1. In 1956, Werner Buchholz coined "byte" for a set of eight bits. The code for a letter or other keyboard character used 1 byte of information, and was the largest amount of data a computer could process at a time. Byte was spelled with a "y" to avoid confusion with bit. In the 1970s, the "nibble" was introduced, named because it had 4 bits and was smaller than a byte, while a "crumb" is 2 bits. Transmitted, or streamed, information is generally measured in bits, while stored information (in computer memory) is measured in bytes.

THE SHANNON

One bit (1 b) of information also equals one shannon (1 Sh). While the bit is a measure of data being handled by a processor, the shannon measures information content of the event. Content is measured as how unlikely, or surprising that bit of information (or string of bits) is. Measuring content helps when considering loss of data during noisy transmissions.

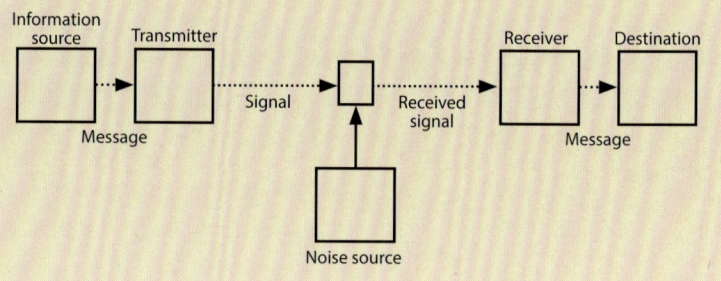

ORDERS OF MAGNITUDE

Information can be counted in both decimal numbers (the ones we use in everyday counting) and as binary (which computers count in). As a result, the normal prefixes that indicate larger quantities, such as thousands and millions, etc, can become a bit confused. For example, "kilo-" normally refers to x 1,000, or 10^3, but it can also mean x 1,024, or 2^{10}. To counter this problem, new prefixes have been introduced for the binary versions as shown in this table, but they are not widely used.

	Decimal				Binary		
2		2 bits		bit (b)		2 bits	2^1
4		4 bits		crumb		4 bits	2^2
8		2 nibbles		nibble		8 bits	2^3
10^3	1000 bytes		kilobyte (kB)	byte (B)	kibibyte (KiB)	1024 bytes	2^{10}
10^6	1000 kilobytes		megabyte (MB)		mebibyte (MiB)	1024 kilobytes	2^{20}
10^9	1000 megabytes		gigabyte (GB)		gibibyte (GiB)	1024 megabytes	2^{30}
10^{12}	1000 gigabytes		terabyte (TB)		tebibyte (TiB)	1024 gigabytes	2^{40}
10^{15}	1000 terabytes		petabyte (PB)		pebibyte (PiB)	1024 terabytes	2^{50}
10^{18}	1000 petabytes		exabyte (EB)		exbibyte (EiB)	1024 petabytes	2^{60}
10^{21}	1000 exabytes		zettabyte (ZB)		zebibyte (ZiB)	1024 exabytes	2^{70}
10^{24}	1024 zettabytes		yottabyte (YB)		yobibyte (YiB)	1024 zettabytes	2^{80}

35 The Turing Test

In 1950, Alan Turing wrote, *Computing Machinery and Intelligence*, in which he proposed a test called the Imitation Game. For a generation, it became the paradigm for understanding artificial intelligence.

In his paper, Turing wondered if it might be possible to build a thinking machine. And if it were, how would we know if it was thinking, and would its thinking be anything like ours? He concluded that it would not be possible to tell a thinking machine apart from a non-thinking machine. Instead, he proposed that it was only important for a machine to appear to be thinking. If a machine did that well enough then it could be regarded as being intelligent. The Imitation Game was a version of a parlor game that was popular at the time. Turing simply recast the game into a test for artificial intelligence (AI).

Three players needed

The game has three players, but only two people. One of the people has the role of interrogator—most often this is actually a jury of people. The other two players are hidden from the interrogator's view. One of them is a computer that is programmed to be a "thinking machine," or AI. The other player is a person. The interrogator asks the players a series of questions. For the sake of fairness, the answers are given as written text. It is the content of the answer, not the quality of the voice, that will win the day. The interrogator (or a majority of the jury) must decide whether A or B is the human. If they get it wrong, then the computer player is deemed to possess artificial intelligence.

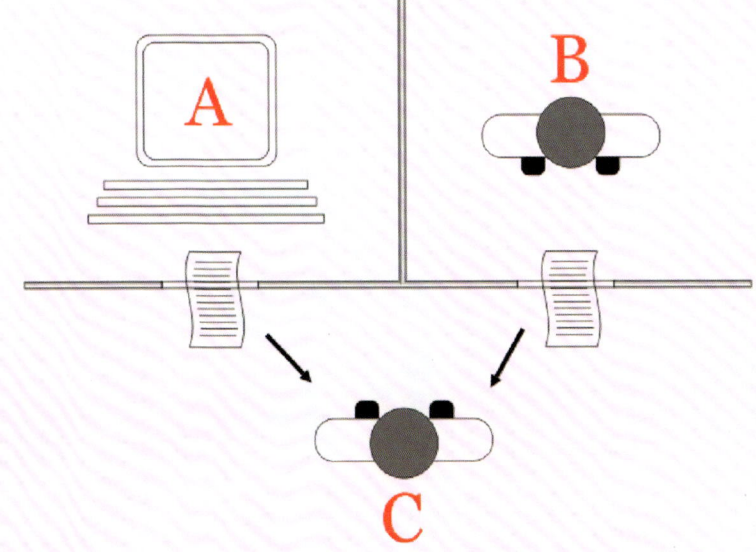

Turing's test is generally carried out by typing questions onto a screen. The interrogator is given five minutes to figure out who—or what—they are talking to.

Programs designed to take the test were called chatbots, and their programmers have employed a range of strategies to fool the judges. One trick was to have the chatbot misspell a few words now and then. That is after all wot a human would do. From the 1990s, Turing test tournaments have been held. Turing had predicted that by 2000, machines would be able to fool a third of humankind through the test. In 2012, 100 years after Turing's birth, a bot called Eugene Goostman, which purported to be a 13-year-old boy from Odessa, Ukraine, was voted as human by a third of the jury. Organizers proposed this met Turing's prediction and so Eugene had passed—the first program to do so. Others disagreed, sticking closer to the rules. Ten years later, large language model AIs, like ChatGPT, passed the test. However, Turing's Imitation Game has proven a failure. We do not yet regard these AIs as thinking machines. Are we wrong?

36 Compilers

A COMPUTER PROCESSOR ONLY HAS THE CAPACITY TO RECEIVE binary information. Data and the controlling algorithm need to be converted into this form, known as machine code, using a program called a compiler.

The first computer programs were written directly into machine code, as strings of 1s and 0s. As programs became more involved, coders developed assembly languages, which replaced chunks of machine code for a specific function with friendlier terms. However, these languages were limited to working on a specific processor. What was needed was a way of converting an algorithm written in a more human-friendly code into the machine code of any computer.

Grace Hopper, the navy officer turned computer pioneer, dubbed such a system a "compiler." In the early 1950s, she and others created different ways of compiling algorithms into machine code. Hopper's system was called A-0. The first true compiler was developed in 1952 for converting programs in Autocode into code for the Manchester Mark 1, a computer that had been developed by a team that included Alan Turing. Compilers are used today to convert the source code in one programming language into any other language, not just machine code.

Software is written in a high-level language using word-like terms to set out the algorithm. It is converted to lower-level codes to work on the hardware.

37 Mainframes

THE FIRST COMPUTERS WERE RESEARCH PLATFORMS RUN BY UNIVERSITIES AND THE MILITARY. As their costs fell and capabilities grew, computers then became business machines—big ones, known as mainframes.

Several corporations—soon nicknamed "IBM and the Seven Dwarfs"—were ready to meet the demand for this new product. The "dwarfs" included Honeywell and General Electric, but no one was able to compete in the space with IBM, or International Business Machines. Thomas Watson, the IBM president, was ready for the challenge. In 1943 he was famously quoted as saying: "I think there is a world market for maybe five computers." (He got that a little wrong. Today, there are at least two computerized devices for every person on Earth.) However, Watson was speaking before the arrival of even the most primitive digital computers in 1946, so we can forgive him. And for several years, Mr. Watson was not far out.

After the relative success of ENIAC, its designers J. Presper Eckert, Jr. and John Mauchly worked on a more powerful computer called EDVAC (Electronic Discrete

Variable Automatic Computer). It was the first to use the binary system rather than the decimal system. (ENIAC was the last one to try that.) The duo then put their technical know-how into UNIVAC I, one of the first computers for the commercial market. It was launched in 1951 and cost a cool $1 million. Only 46 were ever made.

Big Blue

Originally the term "mainframe" meant just the cabinet where the processor and other important components were stored. By the time IBM entered the fray in 1952 with the IBM 701, the huge computers themselves were being called mainframes. The mainframe then took on a totemic meaning. This was the heart of a corporation, a whirring nerve center upon which the enterprise was built. The mainframes lived up to this description through size. Many were built in situ and filled entire floors of a building—once the storage had been installed (see page 50). They cost inordinate sums, and therefore remained few and far between.

In reality, mainframes were chiefly tasked with the mind-numbing tasks required by large corporations: Payroll, accounting, stock control, etc. The IBM 701 was the first in the 700 series, which still used valves, or vacuum tubes, in its logic circuitry. This was the model used by NACA, the precursor of NASA. There was a cheaper, smaller version, the IBM 600 series, which became the first mass-produced computer. By the early 1960s, the mainframes of the upgraded 7000 series were based on those new-fangled transistors. No one saw any particular need to connect these machines—no one, that is, until the U.S. military began to roll out a computer-based air-defense system in the late 1950s. Then people began to wonder what might be achieved by creating a network of the world's best computers.

A team of technicians tends to the UNIVAC Livermore Advanced Research Computer located at the Lawrence Livermore National Laboratory, a U.S. government research facility. The mainframe was completed in 1960 and was 175 times more powerful than the UNIVAC I from nine years before.

38 Memory and Storage

ALONG WITH POWERFUL PROCESSORS, COMPUTER SCIENTISTS developed new and ever more efficient ways to store information.

All computers need a way of storing code. A modern computer has registers in the central processing unit microchip itself that hold values for just fleeting moments as the algorithm executes. Data that is being worked on is also stored temporarily in the RAM, or random access memory, which is a solid-state storage device (SSD)—another kind of microchip. The computer keeps things for the longer term in its storage. In today's devices this is most likely another SSD, but for many decades the go-to storage system was the hard disk drive (HDD). Although slower to read and write to, HDDs are still cheaper and can store large amounts of information, measured into the terrabytes.

HDDs were the product of many innovations in computer storage, beginning with delay line memory that used sound waves. To store more data in more compact devices, computer scientists turned to electromagnetism. Initially, this was done using wire, and then flexible tape covered in iron oxides. Later, this developed into disks of (literally hard) magnetic material. The first was introduced in 1956. (There were also "floppy" disks made from thinner, flexible magnetized plastics.) Each hard disk has several platters, all spinning at up to 15,000 revolutions per minute. A spindle, which is very like the needle of a vinyl turntable, swings to position an electromagnetic "read-write" head in an exact location. To save data, the head magnetizes sectors of the platter—and de-magnetizes others if necessary—to make a pattern that represents 1s and 0s. To read data from the disk, the spindle hangs above the platter, and the magnetized sectors induce a current in the head, while the demagnetized areas do not, and this pattern of currents forms an input of 1s and 0s.

RAM is so-called volatile memory because it only stores data when switched on. On the other hand, a hard disk is an example of non-volatile memory—it holds information even when powered down. HDDs do get full up, so important files are archived onto other non-volatile memory. For example, this store of magnetic tape held the long-term archive of Munich University, Germany.

BULLAE
Physical data storage is not new. People have been keeping a record of important facts for 10,000 years—as long as civilization has existed. Mesopotamians used bullae— hollow clay balls that were filled with tokens representing quantities of animals and food. The bullae were sealed shut as a physical and infallible accounting of a person's wealth or goods.

39 Fortran

ONE OF THE MOST SIGNIFICANT INNOVATIONS IN COMPUTER SCIENCE was the creation of programming languages. The first high-level language was Fortran, designed by IBM for its mainframes. There was a long way to travel, but this was a first step in the long journey to bring computing into the mainstream.

As computers slowly found their way out of the research lab and into everyday use in offices and schools, a skills deficit followed. Only a handful of experts were able to write programs in the correct machine code or assembly languages that the devices used. What was needed was a new programming language that was dislocated from the "low-level" physical operations of the processors and other components. Instead, the new language needed to focus on the abstract concepts used to describe algorithms. These "high-level" items include variables, loops, Boolean operations, and decision-making conditionals. Fortran (short for "formula translation"), released in 1957 by IBM, was the first language to do this. It is still in use today!

Equipped with Fortran, experts of another sort—engineers, businesspeople, and scientists—became the ultimate guides of what their computers were doing. Where once these programs were assembled from about 1,000 unique instructions known only to a few, Fortran users need to only grapple with 47 commands!

John Backus, Fortran's main creator, described the early days of programming as "hand-to-hand combat with the machine," and often ending up on the losing side! Programmers spent half of their time debugging. Backus built an eclectic team with chess enthusiasts, code experts, geologists, and mathematicians. Over four years, the team wrote a language that captured the intent of each step in an algorithm, and created a syntax for it similar to mathematical notation. That syntax could be followed by a human—and also compiled into machine code.

For loading onto a computer, Fortran programs were written as patterns on a punched card like this one, with 80 columns and ten rows.

40 How To Be a Real Hacker

THE IDEA OF HACKING SOON ATTRACTED A SUB-CULTURE OF COMPUTER SCIENTISTS. OF COURSE, it is widely seen today as a malign activity. The original hackers, however, had a different interest—model railways!

To be a hacker is not synonymous with being a computer criminal. Hacking has its origins in a culture of thinking technically, but in a different way. A hack in its purest form is to use a current piece of technology for a purpose that it was not designed for. Today we regard hackers as murky cybercriminals (not without foundation), but the basis of hacking culture grew out of a harmless hobby. In 1955, members of the Tech Model Railroad Club at the Massachusetts Institute of Technology (MIT) were asked not to "hack" while the computer network was powered up. This instruction referred to the way overly eager people who decided to do a bit of rewiring or track changes to improve the railroad set while the trains were running, often blew all the fuses in the process!

A fire truck was mysteriously parked on top of the Great Dome at MIT in a September 2006 hack designed to commemorate the 9/11 attacks.

These early hackers were workers at one of the world's leading technological research institutes, and their methods of thinking and working fast to make rapid and rough changes was infectious. They were doing much the same with the MIT computer systems. Ever since those days, students at MIT have a tradition of thinking of hacks on the grand scale. These are pranks that use the buildings, furniture, or other facilities in novel ways. (The only rule is: Don't break the rules.)

Hacking was part of the culture of software development from the early days. Many of the leaders of the personal computer revolution were hackers with an alternative view on the future of computing. However, an all too obvious way to repurpose software is to use it to steal and destroy. Hacking has become a powerful tool of online criminals, and this activity crowds out its more benign—and useful—features.

> **JARGON FILE**
> By the 1970s, hackers had developed their own language, which they recorded in a dictionary called the Jargon File. Some entries include:
> **Hacker**: A person who explores programmable systems and stretches their capabilities—unlike most users, who prefer to learn the minimum necessary.
> **Sandbender**: A silicon chip manufacturer.
> **Wizard**: A hacker known to be the community's leading authority on a certain topic.
> **Sneaker**: A hacker hired to test cyber security.
> **Cracker**: A criminal hacker intent on doing harm.

41 The Perceptron

IT IS NOW COMMONLY UNDERSTOOD, THAT MODERN AIs, right up to the cutting edge of the technology, make use of "machine learning." They are trained to do a job. This fundamental technology has a surprisingly long history, stretching back 60 years to this device: The perceptron.

A perceptron is a system for classifying data into one of two possible outputs. Such a device—as long as it is accurate in its classifications—is a useful tool for an artificial intelligence making decisions.

The idea for a perceptron goes all the way back to 1943, when Warren McCulloch and Walter Pitts sketched it out in theory. Their plans developed from neuroscience, the study of physical and chemical activity of the brain, itself a young science in the 1940s. The American researchers spotted how certain neurons with only two output connections (most have many more) functioned in a way that could be expressed in simple mathematical logic. A few years later, in 1949, the Canadian neuroscientist Donald Hebb proposed a theory of learning, summarized as "cells that fire together, wire together." In other words, neurons that communicate regularly strengthen their connections. Memory and other brain processes are executed along such cell circuits. The mathematical neurons of McCulloch and Pitt could now be made real and "wired" together. Each connection was given a numerical weight showing its relative strength.

Like Babbage and Lovelace before them, McCulloch and Pitt needed a device to test and develop their mathematical perceptron. That was beyond the technology of the day. A perceptron wired up with artificial neurons had to wait until the days of the transistor. The first was the Mark I Perceptron, constructed at Cornell Aeronautical Laboratory in 1957. It was connected to a primitive digital camera with 400 light-sensitive cells each detecting light at a different intensity. The brain-inspired algorithm could classify simple images, but only those that fell into clearly distinct sets. Any overlap in features confounded the system. Despite its obvious limits, Mark I proved the concept of machine learning, and as AI historians of the future will learn, it was only a matter of time before machine-learning algorithms were improved to see patterns everywhere!

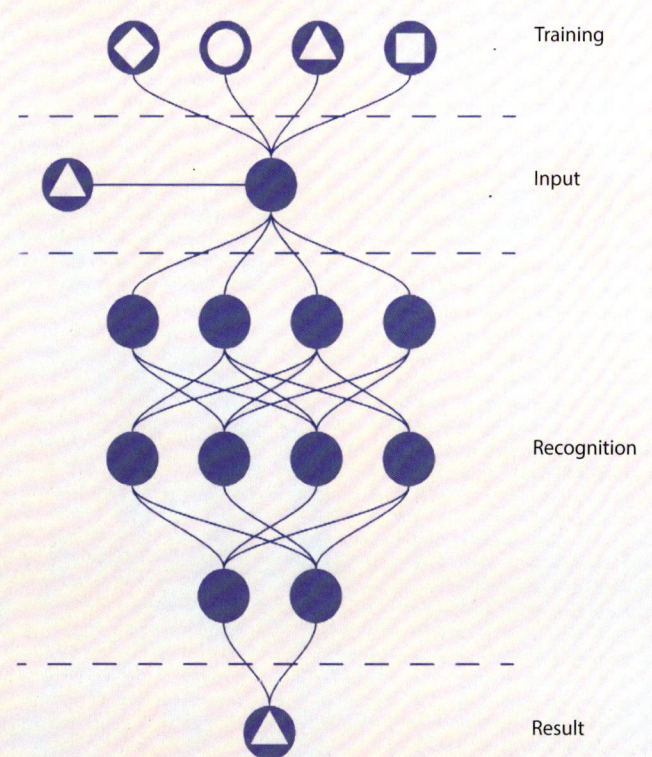

The Peceptron is an early incarnation of an artificial neural network. Based on the filter-like layers of cells seen in the human cerebellum, a neural network classifies inputs into binary outputs, over and over again, to arrive at a final result that is very likely to be true (given enough training).

42 Inventing the Microchip

HOFSTADTER'S LAW STATES THAT EVERY PLAN TAKES LONGER THAN YOU THINK. That rule certainly applies to the development of the transistor-powered computer. One more innovation was needed: The microchip.

The transistor had been invented in 1947, but mainframes were still using processors built from vacuum tubes into the 1960s. What was the hold-up? The answer is that there was still a great deal of innovation needed. A big step was the invention of firmware in 1951. This was a little program that controlled the low-level operations of the central processor unit—so the other programming did not have to. The firmware was stored on non-volatile, or permanent, ROM (read-only memory), and it simplified the future development of CPUs. But these were still being built from valves. (The first commercial use of a transistor was actually in a hearing aid in 1952.)

The first "transistorized" computer was the TRADIC of 1954. It contained 800 transistors and 10,000 rectifiers (for smoothing out current). It was a fraction of the size of ENIAC—about the size of a washing machine—and was 2,000 times faster. Even so, TRADIC was sluggish compared to its vacuum-tube competitors—and still very expensive.

The integrated circuit

The transistor was still an infant technology. One of its inventors, William Shockley, left Bell Labs and was looking for a place to set up a transistor laboratory. His mother was living in Mountain View near San Francisco, so he set up the Shockley Semiconductor Laboratory nearby. That was the simple decision that led to this area becoming the location of Silicon Valley, the heartland of the world's computer industry.

As TRADIC had proved, transistors could be made smaller than valves. The idea was plain enough. Being smaller meant a processor could have more of them, and more transistors meant a faster computer. However, going small created its own set of problems. It was difficult to wire the components together. In 1958, Jack Kilby, working at Texas Instruments, made the big leap. He created an integrated circuit of transistors set up in various, configurations, where all the components and their

A couple of chips are hardwired into a motherboard with other components. The chip is so-called because it is one of several cut from a larger wafer of pure silicon.

connectors were incorporated into the same piece of material. Over at Fairchild Semiconductor around the same time, Robert Noyce made an integrated circuit the size of a pencil point from a single wafer, or chip, of silicon. This was the first "microchip." Microchips took about a decade to develop, and in the interim computers made do with using larger transistors wired on motherboards. The first computer to use a single microprocessor—a processor miniaturized on a chip—appeared in 1971. It had been a 25-year gamble, but the bet on semiconductors would certainly pay off!

Microfabrication

The transistor is the most manufactured item in history, with 13 sextillion made so far—give or take a few quintillion. They are made by a process called microfabrication. A big part of the process is photolithography. The chip is coated in a light-sensitive chemical called photoresist and then covered in a sheet of glass with a master copy of the circuit diagram on it. A powerful ultraviolet light shines through the mask removing any photoresist it hits and exposing the silicon. The exposed silicon now forms the pattern of the final circuit. Next, the surface layer of silicon dioxide is removed in a process called etching. Tiny channels are carved into the circuit pattern and the pure silicon is then doped with chemicals and layered with metallic conductors to build up the tiny transistors and connectors. It is an intricate process. The components are a few billionths of a meter long!

A microchip factory is called a fab. It needs to be clean: Even the tiniest mote of dust would wreck a chip. Fabs have cleanrooms filled with filtered air. Normal air has 35 million particles bigger than 0.5 micrometers in every cubic meter. Filters remove all particles bigger than this before the air gets into the cleanroom.

THE TRAITOROUS EIGHT

Despite being one of its inventors, William Shockley's contribution to semiconductor technology came to a halt in 1957. His semiconductor lab had been running for about a year, crewed by the brightest science minds he could find. The team had a lot to innovate to make transistors a viable product. However, Shockley was not the best boss (and was perhaps mentally ill). Eight of his employees soon had enough. They walked out and set up Fairchild Semiconductor, a rival—and as history records, a superior—operation. The group became known as the Traitorous Eight, because they were seen as building a company on the efforts of Shockley. They did not agree. After all one of the eight was Robert Noyce, who would invent the microchip the following year!

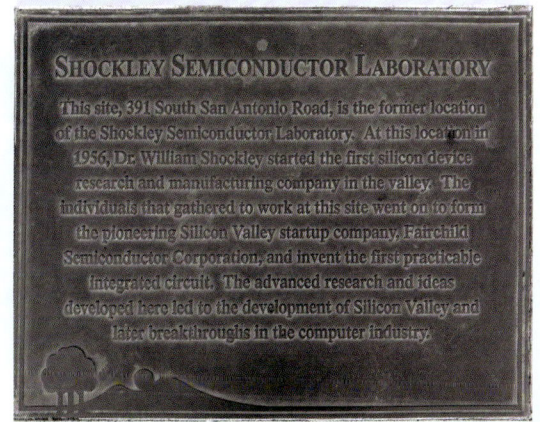

43 Computer Modelling

IN THE 1950S, THE RAW CALCULATING POWER OF COMPUTERS changed the field of mathematical modelling. Computers began to simulate real-world processes and changed our understanding of nature—and math—all at once.

A mathematical model is a description of a natural process using mathematical relationships. Meteorologists could see how to model weather systems from the start point of some observational data, but the mathematics were too arduous to complete in time for the results to be a forecast. The bad weather would have come and gone long before. This all changed with the arrival of digital computers. One of the first jobs of ENIAC was to compute a weather forecast—its accuracy is not recorded! The possibilities were not limited to the weather. In the early 1950s, the detonation of nuclear bombs was modelled by a U.S. military computer called MANIAC. Much better than doing it for real. And in 1963, Edward Lorenz's model of air circulation led to chaos theory, better known as the Butterfly Effect, where tiny changes to the starting conditions can lead to huge swings in possible outcomes. By the late 1960s, the U.S. National Oceanic and Atmospheric Administration began to model the planet's entire atmosphere. That work is still going on, with models being refined to include more data points to increase their accuracy. Today, NOAA's enormously powerful supercomputer models the atmosphere far into the future—and into the past.

It takes about six weeks to calculate by hand six hours of weather. But, by the mid 1950s, computational forecasts were giving results quickly enough for the predictions to be useful.

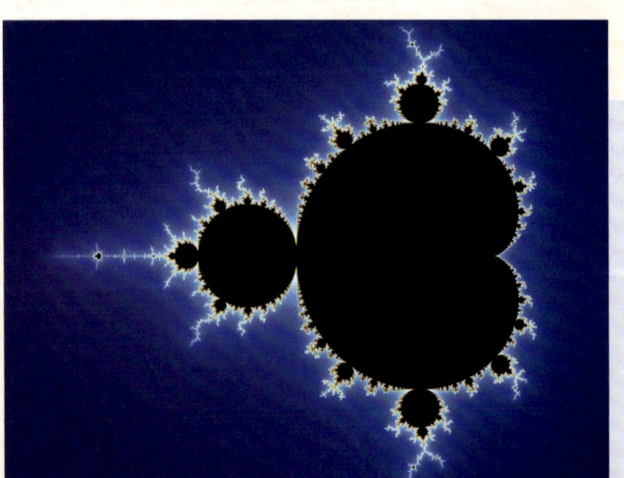

FRACTALS
Derived from the Latin word for "broken," a fractal is a geometric shape that has detailed structures when viewed at any scale. Magnify or move further away, and the shape will not smooth out. It would be impossible to illustrate a fractal's characteristic without a computer calculating its shape at different scales. Sometimes, the same features recur infinitely as the scales change. A famous fractal that does this is the Mandelbrot set, named after the French-American Benoit Mandelbrot, who used an IBM mainframe to visualize it for the first time in 1980.

44 Moore's Law

In 1965, Gordon Moore, a member of the Traitorous Eight, made a prediction about the future of computing that has been true ever since.

At the time, Moore was running research and development at Fairchild Semiconductor, so he knew a thing or two about semiconductors. He said the size of a transistor would halve every 18 months, a statement now known as Moore's Law. In 1968, Moore and Robert Noyce set up the chip-maker Intel, and within a few years chips were standard components in computers. Moore's Law stood up to this first brush with reality, although it is easier to rephrase it to say that every 18 months, processors double in speed because they have ever more of the ever smaller components. In 1970, a transistor was 10 micrometers long and there were 1,000 of them on a microchip. Today, the most powerful chips, like those used in the servers in data warehouses, have a staggering 50 billion transistors! The transistors are between 3 and 4 nanometers (billionths of a meter) across—and they are becoming smaller still! However, there is a physical limit to the size of a transistor below which it cannot work. Moore's Law will eventually come to an end, but when?

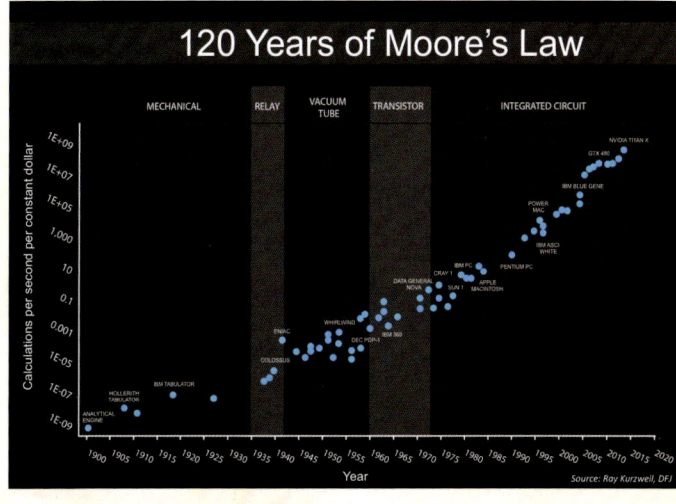

Nothing sums up computer history better than a logarithmic plot of speed of processors through the ages.

45 UNIX

The operating system is the software that manages the input and output devices and other programs being run. Most of them are based on Unix.

Unix is an operating system that was developed in 1969 by Bell Labs as internal software. However, it was so good at its job that in the 1970s the parent company—AT&T, the telephone company—rolled it out everywhere. The movers and shakers of the computer world, from Microsoft to IBM, customized their own versions. Today, most computing devices have an operating system descended from the original Unix. That includes Playstations, Apple Macs, Chromebooks, Android phones, and Linux machines. Windows is the main exception. The Unix "philosophy" is to use robust utility programs for each job and only combine them if needed. Unix also treats "everything as a file." This means, hardware devices and systems information are accessible within the same directory hierarchy as actual files, like emails, photos, and documents.

46 Switching On the Internet

The idea of connecting computers into networks has its roots in military applications. But over half a century after the system went live, the technology has fostered an all-pervading data space that has found its way into every part of our lives and transformed society many times over.

In the late 1950s, with the world nearing the summit of the Cold War, the U.S. military began to roll out a computer-based air-defense system. Airbases, command centers, and early-warning sites were connected by dedicated telephone lines, and modems whistled and twanged top-secret data hither and thither. Soon enough, it became apparent that this defense network was vulnerable to attack. One broken line was enough to cut off assets from their commanders. A few more severed lines—a likely

A map of ARPANET in 1977 covering most of the mainland of the United States and including zigzag satellite links to Hawaii and London.

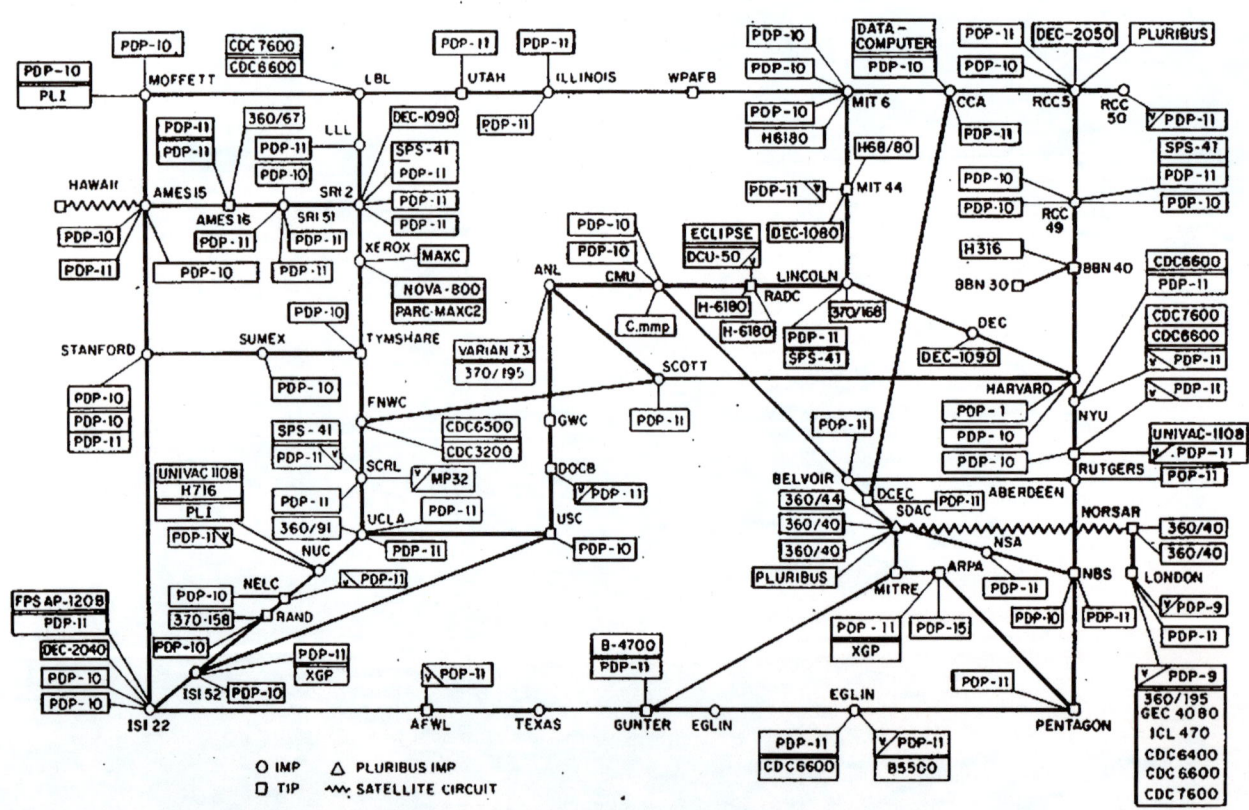

PACKET SWITCHING

A large message is split into thousands of individual, equal-sized "packets" of around 1,500 bytes apiece. Each packet has a header that indicates where it fits in the original message with all the other packets. Every packet takes a different route through the network, directed from node to node, and they are only reassembled in the right order at the final destination. If a packet is missing, the receiver can request it to be sent again. The system will work even when nodes are removed.

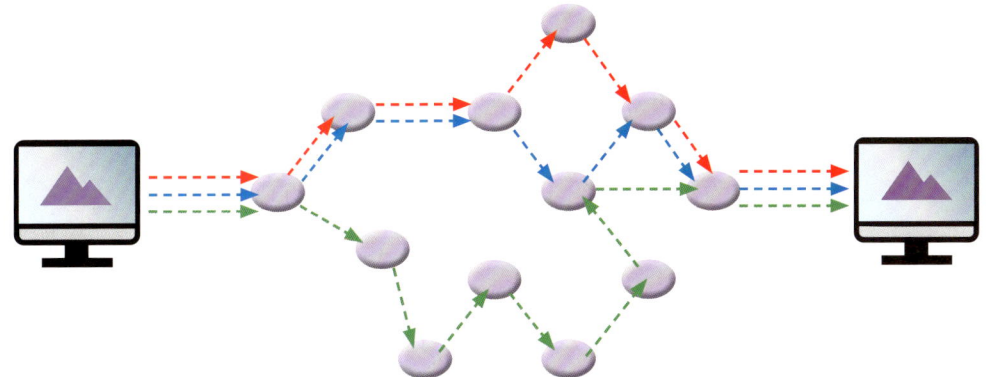

outcome during an enemy attack—would render the system useless. To solve this issue, the U.S. government commissioned the Advanced Research Projects Agency Network, or ARPANET. This involved connecting computers using a distributed network—something more like the civilian telephone network. Then signals sent between computers could find their own way to their destinations via any number of network nodes. If one route was blocked, the message could take another route. This made use of a communications technology called packet switching (see box), devised independently by Lawrence Roberts and Leonard Kleinrock at ARPA, and Donald Davies at the UK's National Physical Laboratory.

A network of networks

In 1969, ARPANET was finally turned on. It was a computer network that linked mainframes at universities, government agencies, and defense contractors around the USA. The first four nodes of ARPANET were UCLA's Network Measurement Center, Stanford Research Institute (SRI), University of California-Santa Barbara, and the University of Utah. On October 29, 1969, the first message ever to be sent over the network was "lo." Student Charles Kline had attempted to type "login," but the system crashed on the "g"! The network grew steadily year on year. In December 1970, the initial ARPANET protocol was completed. Called the Network Control Protocol (NCP), it allowed network users to begin developing applications to run on the network. A key concept was the open architecture of the network. Individual networks could be designed and developed according to their users' needs and then linked into other networks by the "internetworking architecture." A champion of this idea was Robert Kahn, who, along with Vinton Cerf, wrote fresh protocols for the network called TCP/IP (which readers might come across when fiddling with Internet settings). For some, the starting date for the Internet is January 1, 1983, when TCP/IP went live.

Other communication networks were being subsumed into the ever-growing Internet. The Internet is the physical network of cables and nodes through which signals are routed according to the set of TCP/IP rules. Initially, the system was used to send emails and to transfer files. However, by the 1990s, a new technology, the World Wide Web, transformed the Internet into something for everyone (see page 80).

47 Email

ELECTRONIC MAIL, MESSAGES SENT AS DATA BETWEEN CONNECTED COMPUTERS, dates back to the early 1960s. However, these early systems only worked within one network. To connect the world, we needed a sign.

The @ symbol is known as the "at sign" in English, despite attempts in the 1990s to rename it the "strudel." Can you see why?

The closed system of electronic messages, or email, needed an upgrade to work over the Internet. It proved to be the first major network application, providing ARPANET's developers with an easy way of coordinating their activities. The system, created by Ray Tomlinson in 1971, would be largely recognizable to email users today. He devised a way of allowing messages to leave one network, or "domain," and arrive at another, by using identifying addresses with the format "name@domain." Tomlinson wrote the basic email send and read software, and the following year, MIT researcher Lawrence G. Roberts finalized the first email application that was able to list, read, file, forward, and respond to messages. Email really took off, and the potential for "people-to-people" communication was a major reason that the Internet grew so much.

Thanks to email, @ has become a very common character, although the symbol was first added to the standard keyboard in the 1900s, as an abbreviation for "at." However, the @ sign actually has a longer heritage: It featured in a Greek chronicle in 1345 CE!

48 Malware

THE INTERCONNECTIVITY OF COMPUTERS HAS LED TO THIS UNWANTED TECHNOLOGY, known by a portmanteau of "malicious software." Malware runs unseen on computers, with the intent of stealing money or data.

Malware is a problem for everyone. Keeping software up to date will help, and users need to maintain good cyber hygiene to ensure their devices—especially computers—stay clean.

As well as giving the world email, in 1971 Ray Tomlinson also invented something a lot less useful but just as consequential in the new world of interconnected computers: The computer virus. The software was called Creeper. It was designed to copy itself and forward that to another device—and keep on going. It did not damage computers "infected" with it. The first anyone would have known about it was a printed message that said: "I'm the Creeper: Catch me if you can." Creeper could only infect mainframes running a particular operating system—and there were only 28 of them connected to ARPANET at that time! The following year, Tomlinson released Reaper, the first anti-virus software, which deleted Creeper into extinction.

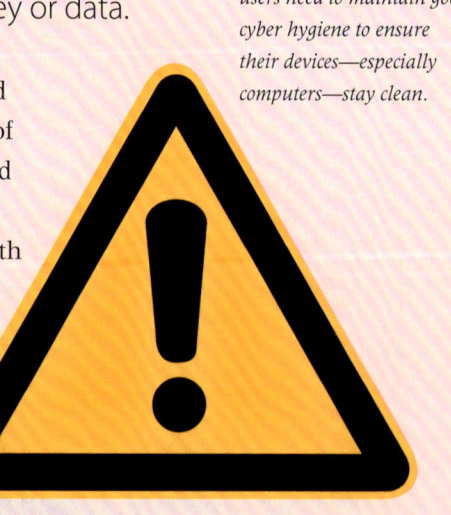

CAPTAIN ZAP

Today, malware is creating billions of dollars worth of losses each year, and causing untold misery for many. A big scam is ransomware, where important documents are encrypted until a ransom is paid. If no money materializes, the documents are made public. In the early days, hackers were perhaps more on our side. "Captain Zap," an anonymous online Robin Hood, is said to have hacked into the AT&T phone company's mainframe and changed the company's internal clock. The result was that AT&T's billing system used the wrong time. Customers were charged night rates during the day and vice versa. This happened back in 1981, the prehistoric days of the Internet, and may all be made up!

Deceptive software

While Creeper has gone, the concept of "malware" was just the beginning. The most familiar type is the computer virus, so-named because it emulates a virus in the way it deploys a computer's own resources to multiply and spread. Generally, a virus is a program that needs to be run by the user so it can install itself on a computer and get to work. It can arrive as an email attachment or be downloaded directly in error. Hackers will use a range of tricks to fool people into clicking on malware. A common trick is to use a Trojan Horse. This appears to be a harmless attachment, such as a picture or document, but once opened, the true contents of the package is released. As historians will already know, the Greek forces used the same trick by gifting the city of Troy a wooden horse. The Trojans pulled the gift within the city's defenses only to find that it contained enemy soldiers! The trick works just as well in modern times. In 2000, 50 million people clicked on an email attachment called ILOVEYOU. Within 10 days, the Love Bug virus hidden within had infected 10 percent of the Internet!

A computer worm is an even more insidious form of malware. Unlike a virus, a worm can spread all by itself, since it uses the software that manages the network to, copy itself and distribute the copies. It will keep multiplying until eventually the network is unable to handle bona fide traffic. One of the oldest malware worms was created by Robert T Morris in 1988—just to see what would happen. The Morris worm exploited a flaw in the way Unix sent emails. The worm was able to infect computers several times over so they stopped working and took days to restore. Causing millions of dollars in damage, Morris was the first cybercriminal convicted in U.S. history. He now has tenure at MIT and was an early investor in start-ups like Airbnb, Twitch, and OpenAI.

PHREAKING

This kind of hack predates the Internet. It makes use of the tones used on the digital phone network. Today each key produces a dual tone, but in the 1950s only one sound was needed. Josef Engressia, nicknamed Joybubbles, had perfect pitch, so he could whistle the notes needed to take control of the telephone exchange at the end of the line—and get free calls. Joybubbles became the first "phreaker" while still a child! (His trick no longer works!)

49 Broadcasting Text

As the world became more connected, what was everyone going to talk about? In the early 1970s, a way of sharing live text information was created. This precursor to websites was hosted not on computers, but on the TV.

The system of broadcast text was first rolled out in the United Kingdom, under the competing names of Teletext and Ceefax. (Similar services appeared in other countries. Two U.S. versions, for example, were called Datavizion and Infotext.) Users would switch to a separate channel—some TV remotes still have a TEXT key devoted to this—and the text would appear on screen. Initially, the TV operated as a dumb terminal, and the viewer would be presented with a series of information screens, switching one to the next. Later, users could access specific screens via an interactive indexing system. Although slow, the teletext was a valued source of news, sports results, weather forecasts, and travel information. The arrival of the World Wide Web in households in the 1990s spelled its end.

Broadcast text gave us a taste of what the World Wide Web could be.

50 The GUI

It is better to read this title as "GOOEY," but the three-letter acronym stands for graphical user interface. Even if you've never heard of the idea, it is hard to imagine the world without it.

Older readers might remember a time when using a computer was a lot less friendly, less intuitive, than it is now. The display—basically a boxy TV set—was blank apart from a blinking cursor and one or two letters in the top left-hand corner. If you pressed keys on the keyboard, characters would dutifully rattle across the screen, colored a tear-inducing green or orange. However, for the untrained user, that was about it. For the computer to do *anything* useful—and that basically meant either write a document or do some sums with a spreadsheet— one needed to command it using

THE MOUSE

The GUI goes hand in hand with the computer mouse. The first one was built by Douglas Engelbart. It was a wooden box with wheels, and the connecting cord originally came out of the front. When that proved cumbersome, the cord was moved to the back, where its tail-like appearance prompted Engelbart to name the device "mouse." Later, the wheels were replaced by a ball. (Below, a 1968 model.)

a series of instructions written in a very particular code. It was nothing too onerous, although it was all too easy to make errors and not so easy to spot them. The system was nevertheless a huge barrier for everyday users, who dismissed computing as something to be left to the experts.

A virtual desktop

The true experts recognized the problem. In the late 1960s, the visionary academic named Douglas Engelbart had the idea for the GUI. This would effectively set the course for the next half-century of computing interfaces, especially for personal computing, until the advent of the smartphone. At the time, Engelbart worked in the Augmentation Research Center (ARC) at the Stanford Research Institute (later SRI International) at Menlo Park in California. In the last weeks of World War II, Engelbart had read about Vannevar Bush's Memex idea and his proposal: A huge postwar initiative to gather and record the world's knowledge. This got Engelbart thinking about the capacity of computers to empower everyone on the planet by providing them with the information they needed to tackle serious problems and improve their standard of living. With this hopeful vision at the front of his mind, Engelbart committed his career to making computers easier to use. The result was the GUI.

In 1968, Engelbart displayed it for the first time at an event that changed the course of computing, now known as the "Mother of All Demos." The team from ARC demonstrated a display screen that was reconfigured as a desktop. And, like a real-world desk, it contained things of importance, not layered as a stack of papers, but as "windows" on screen. Actions were made by pointing the mouse cursor at icons and clicking. No codes were needed.

Building on Engelbart's breakthroughs, the electrical engineer Alan Kay further refined the GUI when he worked at the Palo Alto Research Center (PARC) run by Xerox. Kay developed further GUI features. Commands were selected from drop-down menus at the top of the screen, and files were organized in folders just as they might be in a real-life office cabinet. The Xerox bosses did not see GUI technology as a commercial prospect, but when Steve Jobs and Steve Wozniak, founders of a new company called Apple Computers, visited PARC, they certainly did!

The Xerox Alto, a prototype personal computer from way back in 1973, had a GUI and many of the features of today's personal computers.

51 The Homebrew Computer Club

IT STARTED OUT AS A GANG OF FRIENDS hanging out and chatting about their shared hobby—computing. It ended up being "the crucible for an entire industry."

The club's first meeting was invitation-only. This invite was asking Steve Dompier to attend the first meeting—and perhaps bring his Altair 8800 with him to show everyone. Dompier had managed to program the computer to play music using the sounds the computer made from radio interference!

The Homebrew Computer Club was by no means a regular gathering. It was held in the garage at Gordon French's house in Menlo Park, California, and the members of the club were also from that area in the heart of Silicon Valley. They had world-leading access to computing hardware, something that few like-minded young men (they were all men) would have had elsewhere. Also the name of the group said it all: "Homebrew" was hacking jargon for software that had been modified from the original release.

The members of the club were not teenagers, as one might presume. They were twenty- and thirty-somethings, and proficient software engineers, some working in industry or employed at nearby Stanford, and others just hacking around. For example, one of them was John Draper, a phreaker known as Captain Crunch, who accessed the phone network using a whistle from a cereal box (hence his name).

Along with the host French, the club was founded by Fred Moore in 1975 with the aim of creating an open forum for people interested in making computers more accessible to everyone. The occasion of the first meeting was for the club to take a look at the Altair 8800, a brand new product said to be a "microcomputer."

It is not surprising that two of the club's members, Steve Wozniak and Steve Jobs (invited later by his friend), would go on to set up Apple Computers the following year, with the express intention of selling microcomputers for personal use. Wozniak only began designing the Apple I computer after that first meeting. Other members of the group included Dan Werthimer, who set up SETI, the "Search for Extraterrestrial Intelligence" (they're still searching), Adam Osborne, who later designed the first portable "laptop" computer, and Jerry Lawson, who was a pioneer of home games consoles.

52 Microcomputer

It had no screen, no keyboard, and users had to make their own case, but the Altair 8800 was the first of its kind.

A microcomputer is not only small, but it also has a processor based on a microchip. We do not need that term any more: Just about all computers are microcomputers today. But back in 1975, they were a new idea that was about to get a lot more attention. The Altair 8800 had been launched in 1974, but it began to capture the public imagination the following year. It was sold for a few hundred dollars as a self-assembly kit containing a motherboard, memory boards, and other components. A keyboard and tape player for loading programs through sound came as extras. One person took particular interest. A few months after hearing about the Altair, Bill Gates dropped out of college and set up Microsoft. The company's first product was Altair BASIC, a programming language for the microcomputer. Gates's business idea was that as microcomputers got cheaper and more common, they would all need software. Given that he is one of the richest people on Earth, his strategy certainly proved a good one.

53 Supercomputer

While some computer designers were thinking small, Seymour Cray had other ideas. In 1976 he launched the first "supercomputer."

The Cray-1 design embraced the vision of a 1970s future. It incorporated a C-shaped cushioned bench around the base to cover the wiring and components. The panels covering the tall central towers came in a range of bright colors.

The term supercomputer came into its own in the 1970s. Before then it could be argued that all computers were "supercomputers" in that they were elite devices constructed to take on the toughest tasks. Microcomputers, meant for personal use, changed that idea of what a computer was for. Against this landscape, Seymour Cray (the founder of Cray Research) set about building the world's fastest computers. The first attempt was Cray 1, which proved a huge success— more than 100 were built. Cray's customers used the computer for codebreaking, engineering design and testing, and weather forecasting. It did that with a groundbreaking 64-bit processor (which is now standard) and 300 megabytes of storage. Nevertheless, a modern Android phone is about 150 times more powerful.

54 The Atari 2600

FOR MANY HOUSEHOLDS, THE FIRST MICROCOMPUTER was a console for playing video games. And in the late 1970s, that console was very likely to be an Atari 2600 Video Computer System.

Complete with a wood-effect plastic casing, the Atari 2600 did a good job of fitting into a 1970s home.

A home video games console is a personal microcomputer like any other, only it is set up to do just one thing really well—play games. Plug in the "joystick" controllers, connect it to the TV, and you are all set. The first video console was the Magnavox Odyssey, launched in 1972. But this "closed-circuit electronic playground" ("video game" was as yet uncoined) was a failure due to the cost, and its simple ping-pong game did not inspire the customers.

The customers would have been familiar with arcade games played on specialist, coin-fed machines. The potential of video games had been demonstrated by physicist William Higinbotham way back in 1958. He had wanted to develop an interesting exhibit for the visitors day at Brookhaven National Laboratory in New York, and adapted a small computer and an oscilloscope display to produce a game called Tennis for Two. The "ball" was a dot bouncing back and forth across the screen, but it quickly became the most popular exhibit, with people standing in line to get a chance to play. By the 1970s, arcade games had moved on. A Magnavox console offered a chance to play little more than Higinbotham's dot game, but what people wanted was to play Space Invaders and other arcade favorites at home. Their wish was granted in 1977 with the launch of the Atari 2600 Video Computer System (VCS). The VCS was the first console to feature game software stored on programmable, read-only cartridges that were inserted into the console—and one of those games was Space Invaders!

For a while, the VCS was the high-water mark for consoles, as game-playing shifted to personal computers like the Commodore 64, Sinclair Spectrum, and PCs. Then, Sony led the next wave with the Playstation in 1994, which used optical disks for loading games, and devoted vastly more processing power to generating graphics (see Computer-Generated Imagery, page 74).

ROM CARTRIDGE

Video games—from the Atari 2600 to the Super Nintendo of 1990—loaded games from a ROM cartridge. (ROM means read-only memory: The cartridges' contents was locked.) The cartridge had first been used in the Fairchild Channel F, a rival to the Atari from 1976. (Thanks to its choice of games, the Atari outsold it by 100 to 1.) The lead developer of the cartridge was Fairchild's Jerry Lawson, one of the original members of the Homebrew Computer Club.

55 How Do Touchscreens Work?

For much of its history, a computer was a "lean-forward" device. It was invariably positioned in a workstation and people would have to come to it to use it. The touchscreen, first invented in 1977, would change all that—eventually. So, today, the computing experience has a lighter touch.

When the first touchscreens appeared in the 1970s and 1980s, they seemed almost magical to people used to typewriters and computer keyboards. Those first screens seeded the idea of tablet computers and smartphones, where the screen works as both the input and output device. Simply touching the computer display to type words or highlight data was the vision of Sam Hurst, a physics professor at the University of Kentucky. Hurst had been thinking about alternative ways to interact with a computer, and came up with a screen activated by being pressed with a pen-like stylus. He set up a company, Elographics, to develop the idea. The initial idea was a transparent screen that would sit on top of the display. The overlaid screen detected the position of the stylus and those inputs were used to change what was seen on the display.

Pressure-based

In 1977, Elographics came up with a more elegant alternative, and the first proper touchscreen. This used layers of transparent conductive material carrying an electrical charge. When the layers were pressed together, they completed the circuit and registered a location on the screen. This is called a resistive touchscreen, and it is a tough design still used today in public touchscreens.

Personal devices, like a phone, use capacitive touchscreens, where the electrostatic charge of the screen is changed by the conductivity of a finger. Touchscreens grew increasingly common with the emergence of the first smartphones and tablets in the 1990s. However, it took the marketing muscle of Apple to make them everyday items, first with the iPhone, and then the iPad. Today, more than two-thirds of us use only a touchscreen device for our computing needs.

Touchscreens are everywhere. We use them to check in at doctors' surgeries and airports, to withdraw money from ATMs, or even to order food from menus in fast-food restaurants. In this way, touchscreens have brought the computer out of the workstation to take a place in all parts of the built environment.

56 Encryption: The Basics

THE INTERNET IS A SYSTEM DESIGNED FOR SHARING INFORMATION, with everyone's data traffic treated equally. But how can we keep our secrets from going public in a very big way?

It is impossible to prevent eavesdroppers from picking up secret communications or collecting sensitive information moving through the Internet. So, the only method to protect data is through the use of codes, or encryption. Secret codes work well because they use "keys" to encode messages. Anyone with the key can access the messages, so the keys must be kept top secret. However, that creates a conundrum. How do we then share secret keys using public Internet connections?

One-way math

Early work on mathematical data encryption dates back to 1874, when mathematician William Stanley Jevons developed operations that were relatively easy in one direction, but reversing the process was much more difficult and disproportionately time-consuming. A little over a hundred years later, cryptographers came up with a version suited for use on the Internet. Whitfield Diffie and Martin Hellman created the Diffie-Hellman key exchange. Suppose that two people, Alice and Bob, wish to send secret messages to each other. They share a lockable box, but have their own padlocks, and their own keys to those padlocks. Alice asks Bob for his open padlock. Placing the message in the box, Alice locks it with Bob's padlock and sends the box to him. Bob uses his own key to open the padlock and access Alice's secret message. Eve, an eavesdropper, could snatch the box as it travels to Bob, but without his private key Alice's message stays secure.

To complete the analogy, the "padlocks" and "keys" are both just big numbers. The

MERSENNE PRIMES

There is a special set of prime numbers named for the 17th-century French monk Marin Mersenne, who first described them. A Mersenne prime (M_p) is one less than 2^p, where p is another prime. There are only 51 known M_p, and they are useful because they are good for making encryption keys.

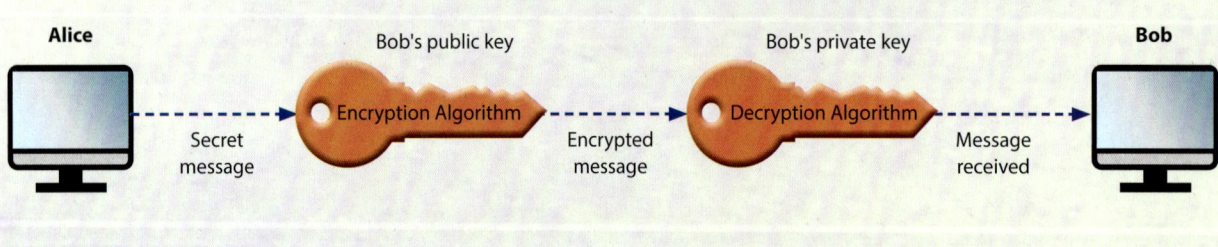

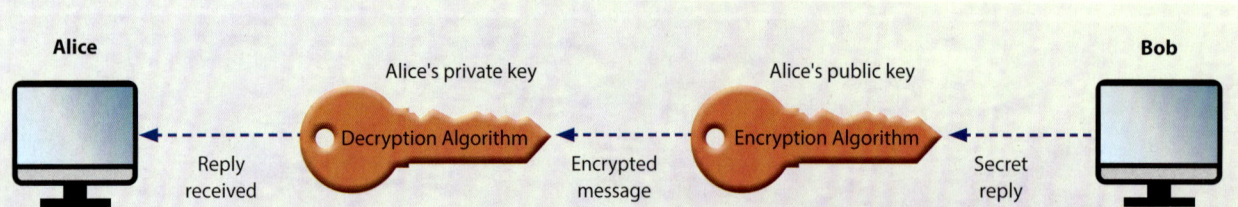

This is a summary of the RSA algorithm (see page 69) sending messages back and forth. When seen this way, it does not appear very different from the Diffie-Hellman method. While RSA is technically less secure than the Diffie-Hellman method (which is a very high bar!), the RSA algorithm allows for both parties to authenticate the identity of correspondents. Diffie-Hellman is used to secure general connections to websites, while RSA is behind more consequential financial exchanges.

padlock number can be sent in public, under the gaze of Eve. It is created using the key number, which is always private and *never* transmitted. Bob is the only person to have both numbers, and that makes decoding the message—or "opening the box"—relatively easy for him. However, Eve has only the public number, so the message stays safely locked in the box.

Prime targets

In 1977, three MIT computer scientists, Ron Rivest, Adi Shamir, and Leonard Adleman created the RSA algorithm, another method of public-key encryption. In the RSA, the public key is a very big number produced by multiplying two large prime numbers. (The Diffie-Hellman system uses primes as well, but in a different way.) The primes are never made public; only Alice knows them. Bob does not need to know them. He uses the public key to encrypt his message and sends that coded information to Alice—again, this is in full view of Eve. Alice uses her private key, which is based on the same initial primes used to create the public key, to decrypt Bob's message. The primes are the only factors of the public key, and so it seems that Eve only needs to figure out, or factor, what those primes are to crack the code.

However, public key encryption relies on the fact that there is no efficient means of factoring large numbers. A snooper would have to try every possible prime number. Eve might eventually succeed in decrypting the message, but it would take months with the fastest computers and the lowest level of security. Today, the best online security uses 128- and 256-bit encryption. In 128-bit encryption, someone hoping to guess the correct number to decipher the secret message would have to work through 2^{128} permutations. A brute force attack (working through every possible permutation) could take 149 trillion years. A 256-bit key would take that amount of time, squared!

PASSWORD STRENGTH

How secure are your passwords? While a criminal or enemy is unlikely to guess your passwords outright, your chosen phrases may be vulnerable to attacks. The simplest is the dictionary attack, where a hacker will try out every word in the dictionary. Adding numbers, capital letters, and symbols prevents this, but there is always a "brute force" attack, where every possible combination of characters is tried. There are 94 characters allowed in passwords, which helps, but the length of the password is the crucial factor. The number of possible permutations of a password with n characters is 94^n. With every extra character, a brute force attack has to do 94 times more work. Adding several would make brute force impossible.

instantly decoded: **1234**

7 quadrillion years to decode: **W2@^prt0£BvBn%2Zx9**

Number of characters	Numbers only	Lowercase letters	Upper & lower letters	Numbers, upper & lower letters	Numbers, upper & lower letters, symbols
4	instantly	instantly	instantly	instantly	instantly
5	instantly	instantly	instantly	instantly	instantly
6	instantly	instantly	instantly	1 sec	5 secs
7	instantly	instantly	25 secs	1 min	6 mins
8	instantly	5 secs	22 mins	1 hour	8 hours
9	instantly	2 mins	19 hours	3 days	3 weeks
10	instantly	58 mins	1 month	7 months	5 years
11	2 secs	1 day	5 years	41 years	400 years
12	25 secs	3 weeks	300 years	2k years	34k years
13	4 mins	1 year	16k years	100k years	2m years
14	41 mins	51 years	800k years	9m years	200m years
15	6 hours	1k years	43m years	600m years	15bn years
16	2 days	34k years	2bn years	37bn years	1tn years
17	4 weeks	800k years	100bn years	2tn years	93tn years
18	9 months	23m years	6tn years	100tn years	7qd years

57 The Origins of AI

TURING'S 1950S MUSINGS ON AI AND HIS TEST FOR THINKING MACHINES certainly got people thinking. A period of optimism about AI began, only to be brought up short in 1980, when John Searle, a philosopher, stepped into the debate. Searle's interventions put AI on its modern trajectory.

It once seemed natural that computer science would one day create artificial intelligence that matches our own. However, while AI already supersedes specific human capabilities, it may be that artificial people who think and behave like us will never be possible.

Like all major technologies, artificial intelligence (AI) has many key milestones. Perhaps the first is the "Dartmouth Workshop" of 1956, where IBM got together a crew of mathematicians and scientists for several weeks at Dartmouth College in New Hampshire. (IBM called it the Dartmouth Summer Research Project on Artificial Intelligence.) The group's job was to figure out how best to begin the process of developing AI. It was agreed that the best approach was to use symbolic logic, a mathematical way of inferring conclusions from premises. The computers were more than capable of handling this kind of information, so what was needed was a master algorithm where intelligence was rendered into a set (admittedly a large one) of logical rules. A big job for sure, but it was presumed that within a generation, logical thinking machines would be our near equals. If only it were that simple—but it proved a lot more complicated! A machine that can think or act rationally does not simulate human thought and behavior. And constructing a machine that thought and acted like a human repeatedly defied the analytical, symbolist approach.

Types of AI

The 1980s rolled around and AIs were still limited to rather repetitive chatbots and expert systems working off a database created and maintained by humans (the real experts). John Searle's 1980 article "Minds, Brains, and Programs," gave some insight into a wider problem with the way computer scientists, with a background in mathematics and engineering, were attempting to develop AI.

Central to his theme was that the Turing Test was by no means a way to prove intelligence. To illustrate this point, Searle made the Chinese Room Argument. Here is a simplified version of this thought experiment. A human operator is sitting in a windowless room with the door locked. There is no way to see into the room from the outside, but there is a slot in one wall for receiving inputs. On the opposite side there is hatch for outputting answers. The operator has a book of instructions. In Searle's setup, this book is for processing inputs made in Chinese characters. Searle no doubt chose Chinese because back then few people in America would have been familiar with it. It could have been Egyptian hieroglyphs or Mayan writing. The point is that the operator does not understand the symbols. However, they look them up in the book and follow the instructions to generate the appropriate response, which they output from the room. Outside, the interlocutors, who can understand Chinese, are thrilled with the room's response. To them the person inside is fluent in Chinese.

Now Searle requests that the human operator is replaced with a machine algorithm that uses the same set of rules to do the job. Outside the room, no one can tell the difference between the human and the machine. Therefore, according to the rules of the Turing test, the machine operator is deemed to qualify as an artificial intelligence.

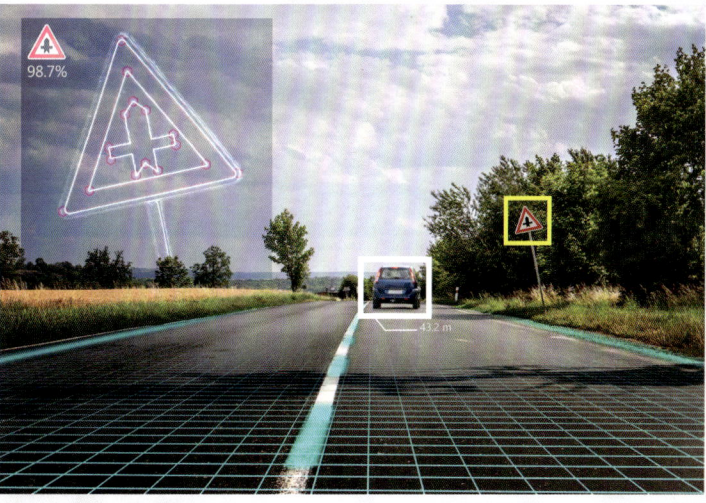

Narrow AI has proven to be very good at recognizing patterns—in images, video, and data. It can be trained through machine learning to "see" the features of a road, but it does not enjoy the view.

Narrow, not strong

Can we really say that the machine inside the Chinese Room is of equal intelligence to the human operator? The former is only able to follow one set of rules; it has no conception of anything beyond this task. Searle described this as a narrow AI. Narrow AI may outstrip a human's ability to do a certain job, but that is all it can do and it will never learn otherwise. Meanwhile, the human can perform the task, but is aware of their ignorance. They know what they do not know (and can learn Chinese if they choose). Searle called this general intelligence. Artificial general intelligence (AGI) has so far eluded developers. To date, all AI is narrow and some doubt AGI is even possible.

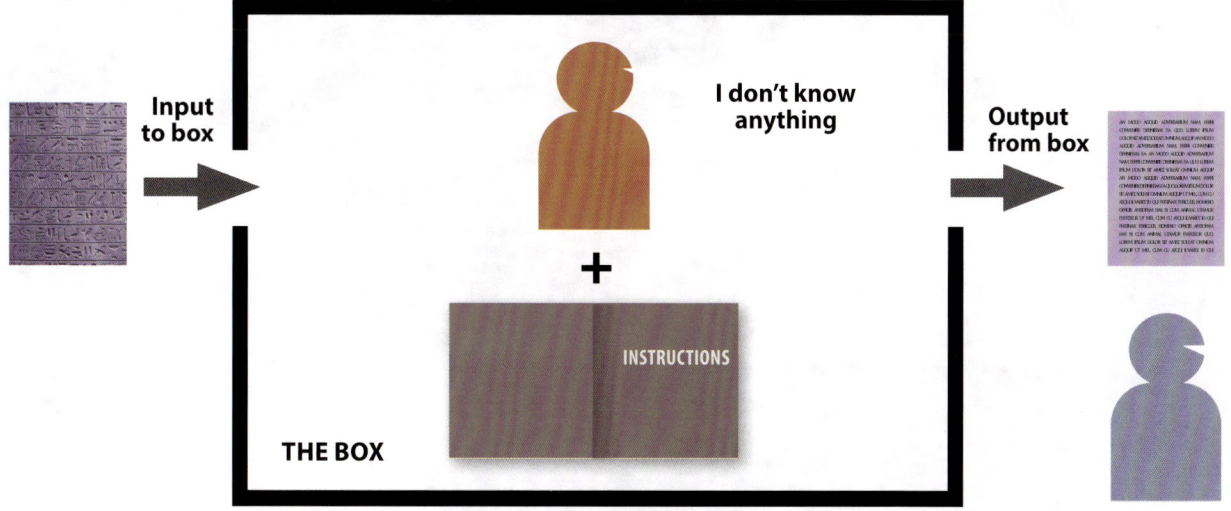

The Chinese Room is a thought experiment designed to illustrate the mismatch between behaving intelligently and being intelligent.

58 Laptops

THE OSBORNE 1 WAS WAY AHEAD OF ITS TIME, but 1981 it led the way for personal computers that work anywhere.

It weighed nearly 25 pounds (12 kg), cost around $6,000 in today's money, and had a display screen that was only 5 inches (13 cm) across, but the Osborne 1 had something. Adam Osborne, its creator, and another member of the Homebrew Computer Club, had imagined a completely portable computer for the busy business executive. It was the first computer that could fit under an airline seat, and on landing you could set it up anywhere (as long as there was an electrical plug nearby). The hard plastic casing and chunky design meant it did not quite qualify as a laptop. Instead, the Osborne 1 was described as a "luggable" computer. Successors soon appeared that cut their weight and size by using flat-screen, liquid-crystal displays. Osborne 1 came with a bundle of applications, including a word processor and spreadsheet. These were all loaded from a stack of floppy diskettes.

With the lid closed, the Osborne 1 looked much like a portable sewing machine, but unclip that cover and a state-of-the-art business machine was revealed.

59 Personal Computers

THE ARRIVAL OF THE MICROPROCESSOR AND THE ENSUING MICROCOMPUTER was a clear signal that the computer was going personal. It would become a product that everyone bought. Who would win in the race to market?

The story of the personal computer is big enough to have spawned movies, novels, and entire museums. There are many twists and turns and missed opportunities, but at its heart the story is the battle between radical thinkers taking on the might of the computer establishment, namely Big Blue, or IBM.

Throughout the 1970s, IBM was developing microcomputing products—and so were a lot of rivals. These devices were targeted at business use, for the home enthusiast, and as a games machine. By the late 1970s, three products, the TRS-80 from Radio Shack, the PET from Commodore, and the Apple II, had emerged as the leaders in this small but growing market. Could they hold on to their lead?

In 1981, IBM released the IBM Personal Computer, better known as the PC. It was designed primarily for use as an office machine but it would do the job anywhere.

The PC was not much more expensive than the Apple II, its chief rival, and had a processor almost five times more powerful. One of 50 similar products launched at around that time, the PC proved a huge success, with at least 50 percent being bought retail rather than wholesale by corporations. To that success was added the system's open architecture. This meant that other manufacturers could build PCs on license from IBM, using cheaper chips and other components. By 1984, most PCs were "clones" rather than IBM originals.

The only true rival left was Apple, where Steve Jobs had a firm control. In 1984, Apple launched the Macintosh, another step change up from the PC. Its GUI and mouse revolutionized desktop computers, and its fast processor and graphics card meant it carved out a niche in design and publishing industries that remains to this day. Even so, by the late 1990s, more than 90 percent of personal computers were PCs, although IBM was in decline. Then Jobs reimagined the product all over again with the iMac. Apple computers and PCs are still the only shows in town, but Apple has migrated to luxury products, which means that although 80 percent of personal computers are PCs, Apple is the largest company in the world and 10 times the size of IBM.

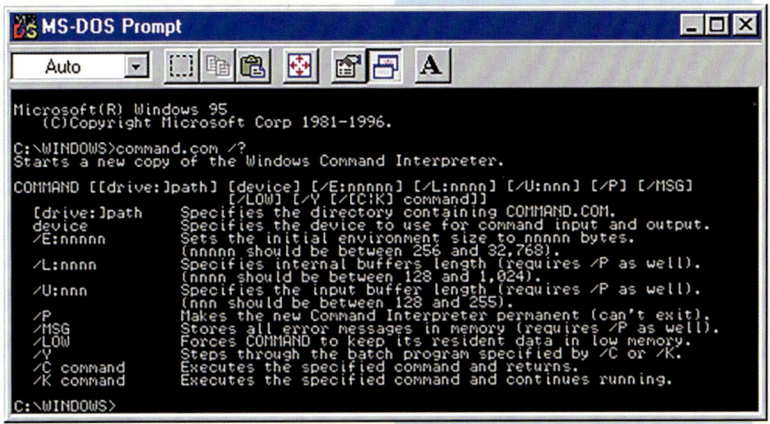

An original IBM Personal Computer, or PC, with keyboard and monitor from 1981. The cost was $5,250 in today's money. Nowadays, an equivalent desktop computer would cost a tenth of this price.

MS DOS

The downfall of IBM was not wholly the doing of Steve Jobs. Bill Gates and his colleagues at Microsoft did a lot more to bring down Big Blue. IBM saw the PC as a hardware product, and that would be how they would profit in the same way that mainframes had made them the biggest computer company. IBM's own-brand PCs used an operating system called PC DOS, but Microsoft had the license for the software on PC clones, and used their own MS DOS. Gates's strategy was that software was the way to make money out of computers, and as the numbers of PC clones steadily swamped the IBM models, he was proven correct. Microsoft launched Windows, a GUI to rival the Mac's, in 1985. Ten year later, Gates was the richest man in the world.

60 Computer-Generated Imagery

IN 1982, COMPUTER SCIENCE MADE IT TO THE SILVER SCREEN, and it did it in two ways at once. Not only was *Tron*, a sci-fi blockbuster, about a programmer trapped in a mainframe, but also much of the action seen on screen was not captured on film. Instead, it was created by a computer.

The first movie to use computer-generated imagery (CGI) was actually Alfred Hitchcock's *Vertigo* in 1958, which featured 2D animated patterns that were added to frames in the film's opening sequence. However, *Tron's* CGI was as much a character in the film as its human stars. Entire scenes were CGI-only, and the live action was overlaid with graphics to create the look of a cyberspace world. Of course, this is nothing now. Entire movies are CGI today, including photorealistic ones that look like they were shot with cameras. The rise of CGI in movies, video games, and in other applications like engineering and architectural design, goes hand-in-hand with a particular kind of microchip, called the GPU, or graphical processing unit. The GPU's job is to perform a lot of complex mathematics fast (see box, right). All computers—and smartphones, too—have GPUs now. (They are not just for rendering displays. GPUs are used for other tricky math in mining cryptocurrency, and more recently as accelerators in AI development.)

The digital skeletons of Sulley and Mike take shape for their appearance in the 2001 animated movie Monsters Inc.

QUATERNIONS

Computer-generated images that model three-dimensional structures in space need a kind of mathematics called quaternions. To show each structure spinning means rendering a moving two-dimensional image on screen as the background moves around it. That means calculating not just the changes in three spatial dimensions, but also their rotation—and doing it fast. The quick way is quaternion multiplication. The CGI is described using complex numbers made up of values in four number lines (hence the term quaternion). Those number lines are 1, i, j, and k, which all translate from one to the other as they multiply, effectively spinning in a space full of numbers to show how the CGI spins in cyberspace.

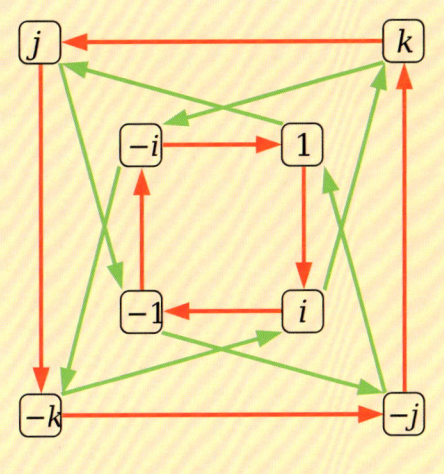

The creation of CGI in movies and games has several steps. First off, artists use specialized software to create 3D models of objects. These models are then given textures, so they have the right look. Each texture is prebuilt, so it distorts in appropriate ways as the model moves. Those movements are preset using a process called rigging, where the joints and range of motion are set within a digital skeleton. Animators then use the rigged models to create sequences, which are processed by the computer to produce the final image or sequence of images. Rendering calculates how light interacts with the objects and environment to create realistic visuals. The final stage is compositing, where images are combined with live-action.

61 Open Source Software

COMPARED TO MICROSOFT AND APPLE, Richard Stallman, a prodigious AI researcher at MIT, had a very different view on how software should be created and owned.

Linux has a penguin called Tux as a mascot.

When we click "Agree" as we install or update our software, we are receiving a license to use that code. It does not belong to us, and we will have paid somehow for the right to use it. This is how software companies got so wealthy. In 1983, Stallman created the GNU Project to make software differently. Code shared under a GNU license is free to run, copy, and rewrite! GNU stands for "GNU's Not Unix." Stallman liked the way the GNU name recurs forever within the phrase. The main aim of the GNU Project was to create a free operating system that was compatible with Unix-based systems. But it was not going to be Unix, which has more than 900 corporate owners. Progress was slow; few coders with the right expertise were putting in the time. Finally, in 1992, Linux, named for its Finish creator, Linus Torvalds, was released under a GNU license. Linux is used by Android phones, and so is the most widely used operating system of all!

62 Optical Fibers

TRAFFIC TRAVELS THROUGH THE INTERNET AT THE SPEED OF LIGHT. It moves as a flickering laser beam that zigzags through a flexible strand of pure silica glass, better known as an optical fiber.

The laser bounces along inside the fiber by total internal reflection. It never shines out through the side of the fiber, only the tip.

The Internet was built from copper wires. Thick cables made from twisted metal, called coaxials, formed the Internet backbones—the name for the big connections within the Internet. Then the service reached the computer in a house or office along a single copper telephone line. In the 1980s, that began to change. The major links were the first to be converted to faster and more efficient optical fibers. There are now 10 million miles (16 million km) of it on the seafloor alone. The biggest cables carry 100 billion bits a second. The idea of sending data by laser this way was formed in the 1960s, but it took a decade or two to perfect the material properties of the fibers. Since then, optical fibers have been spreading out from the backbones, into neighborhoods and, increasingly, to the door of every home. Fiber optic cable is at least 1,000 times faster than copper (although your Internet provider will seldom upgrade your service by that much)!

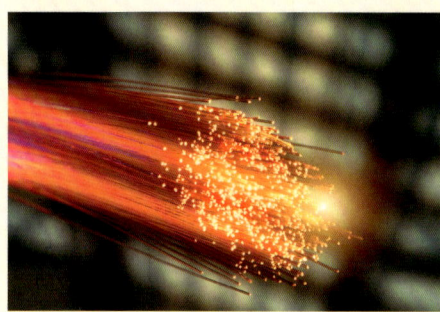

63 Self-Driving Cars

THE FIRST CARS WERE KNOWN AS "HORSELESS CARRIAGES," so it is possible that driverless cars might be called something very different in years to come. The journey to autonomous vehicles began in the 1980s and there is still a long road to travel.

Driverless cars are currently referred to by their creators as autonomous vehicles, or AVs. History will tell if this name sticks. Work on AVs began in Pittsburgh in 1984. Those "Navlab" vehicles were converted vans—they needed the space inside for all the computer hardware. They relied heavily on GPS to tell them where they were. Forty years later, after years of testing, the first AVs are out on public roads, working as robotaxis. They are run by the likes of Waymo, a Google-owned venture, and Uber, and are becoming a common sight on the streets of San Francisco, California, and Phoenix, Arizona. Several other cities also plan to allow the service. The AVs are

How long will it be until everyone in a car is a passenger? Experts suggest most cars will keep their steering wheels until at least 2035.

SMOOTHER DECISIONS

Autonomous vehicles rely on a system called fuzzy logic to make decisions. Precise information about the real world is not always the best way to understand what is happening, so fuzzy logic is able to classify facts as being more than one thing. For example, the weather can be classed as both sunny and cloudy, with a weighting given to each one. This way of seeing the world helps "smooth out" the actions of a car and other AIs.

An AV uses cameras, lidar, radar, and ultrasonic sensors to build up a picture of the road. A computer processor on board uses an AI algorithm to interpret the data and move the car safely from A to B.

- Long-range radar senses car in front
- Forward lidar scan detects pedestrians and other unexpected obstacles during an emergency
- Camera checks traffic signals and road markings
- Anti-collision radar
- Surround-view cameras
- Ultrasonic proximity sensors
- Blind spot radar
- Rear collision warning
- Rear camera

programmed to be very cautious, and to date there have been few accidents. However, human road users complain that the robotaxis are just bad drivers. They are likely to stop in the middle of the road, and during complex situations their maneuvers can disrupt the flow of human drivers. In other words, they cut you up. The robotaxis use a narrow AI to control their actions. Will they get smarter or will AVs always be bad drivers on busy urban roads?

Self-driving vehicles still use GPS to place themselves on the map, so they can navigate routes and change lanes for turns and intersections. However, GPS is not able to show the car what is around it, such as other road users, pedestrians, road signs, and traffic signals. For that the cars use a combination of live video, radar, a laser-based scanner known as lidar, and ultrasonic sensors. The video is provided by cameras pointing front and back, and side to side. The AI will identify what can be seen in each view, differentiating between a car, a cyclist, a pedestrian, and a road sign. This job is aided by the lidar, which gives information about the distance to each object and their speeds and direction. Ultrasonic sensors are used to check the proximity of passing cars. Keep looking at the road ahead. Soon the car in front will be driving all by itself.

64 Printing for All

IN THE MID 1980S, THE WORLD WAS STILL RUN ON PAPER. A printed hard copy of a document or image was its most authentic (and official) version. In 1984, two new technologies brought printing into the home.

Early printer technologies emulated the action of a typewriter. They relied on the impact of inked type or other actuators to leave a mark on the paper. A daisy-wheel system had letters, numbers, and other characters on a wheel that swivelled this way and that to type out words—but it could not print pictures. The dot matrix printer assembled all characters from patterns of smaller dots, and could therefore create shapes as well. However, neither text nor pictures made from these small but visible dots was comfortable to the eye.

By 1984, two better options became available to the home user, as well as office workers, and those two options remain largely the same today: A laser printer or an inkjet system. Both survive because of their different set of advantages. Laser printers are fast and can produce large print runs very cheaply. They are, however, best at outputting text and simple black and white images. Color laser printers do exist and create images of amazing quality—but at amazing costs as well! Inkjets are slower and the cost of the ink means they are more expensive for printing text than laser printers. However, they are a cheaper alternative for high-resolution color prints.

Inkjets build text and images from tiny dots of ink—too small to see with the naked eye. These dots are propelled from the print head by heating ink inside so it expands, forcing out a droplet. Laser printers create a pattern of charge on a drum that matches the pattern of the printed material. A charged toner powder then clings to the drum and is transferred to the paper. Finally, heat seals the toner to the paper.

Color printers of any kind need four inks, or toners. This follows the CMYK, or cyan, magenta, yellow, and black (the K), system. These four tones can be mixed in specific ways to create any shade of color. The extra toners needed make color printing much more expensive than using just black ink.

3D PRINTER

In the mid-1970s, engineers realized inkjet technology could be used for more than just ink. Instead of spraying spots of ink, the printer could produce tiny drops of liquid rubber, plastic, or another material that would solidify. The printer would then continue to build a three-dimensional object, layer by layer. One day houses might be printed with liquid concrete, and even biological material can be printed this way!

65 MS Office

WHY DOES A PERSON EVEN HAVE A COMPUTER? In the end, it is to use the applications—the programs that do useful things. In 1990, Microsoft showed the world how applications were at the heart of computing.

1990 was the year that Microsoft Office was launched (now often shortened to Ms Office). This was a suite of applications that included a word processor (Word), a spreadsheet (Excel), and a presentation designer (Powerpoint). Back in the 1990s, in a world where the Web was very much in its infancy, these products were what computer users purchased their PCs for in the first place. They have remained at the heart of what people use their computers for every day for work and study. All these years later, those three applications are still the main offerings in the software package. Even people who run Apple computers instead of PCs will buy Office to access them. (Remember, PCs almost universally will run on a Microsoft operating system called Windows, while Apple computers use a Unix-based one. Even so, Apple customers are often Microsoft customers as well. That is the power of a good application.)

What is an application?
A computer application—or just "app"—is a type of software built so people can use their computer for a specific task. For example, a word processor turns the computer into a device for creating written documents. A spreadsheet makes it a data analysis tool, and with the advent of Web connectivity, we now also use entertainment apps like games and video players that turn our computer into a cinema screen or TV. The Office applications of the 1990s were for desktop or laptop computers, so are described as desktop applications. Some applications come in a pre-installed bundle, which is still a powerful driver for choosing which computer to buy. When applications are transferred to a mobile device, everything gets smaller and a bit simpler—even the name. That's why we refer to them as mobile apps. There is an app for everything, the saying goes, and each year $160 billion is spent worldwide on mobile apps alone!

The Microsoft Office suite of applications has grown over the decades. It now includes the OneDrive cloud storage system, Outlook email, and Teams videoconferencing. Then there's Yammer, a messaging platform; SharePoint, a document management system; and OneNote (the N above) which is a note-taking application. What will be next?

66 The World Wide Web

THE INTERNET WAS BUILT TO CONNECT COMPUTERS. At first, these were the "big iron" mainframes of large institutions, but by the 1980s, personal computers were connecting. What was needed was a new way of searching and sharing all the information available on the Net.

When Tim Berners-Lee joined the particle physics laboratory at CERN in Geneva, Switzerland, in the 1980s, the British software engineer was struck by how difficult it was for the many scientists working there to share information. The best way was to chat about projects over coffee. But Berners-Lee also knew that every aspect of CERN's many projects was stored on hundreds of computers dotted around the site. The computers could be physically connected, but there was little guarantee that a neighboring device used the same operating system or stored its data in a way that another computer could access. The solution that Berners-Lee came up with for this problem became the World Wide Web. For many of us today, the Internet has become synonymous with the Web, because we consume all the Internet has to offer through the framework created by Berners-Lee all those years ago.

Linking information

In March 1989, in a document called "Information Management: A Proposal," Berners-Lee, with help from his colleague Robert Cailliau, laid out his ideas. It was based on hypertext, a means of linking stored documents using embedded clickable words. Essentially, this was Vannevar Bush's Memex idea

Tim Berners-Lee is now the head of the World Wide Web Consortium (W3C), which oversees the software standards used on the Web.

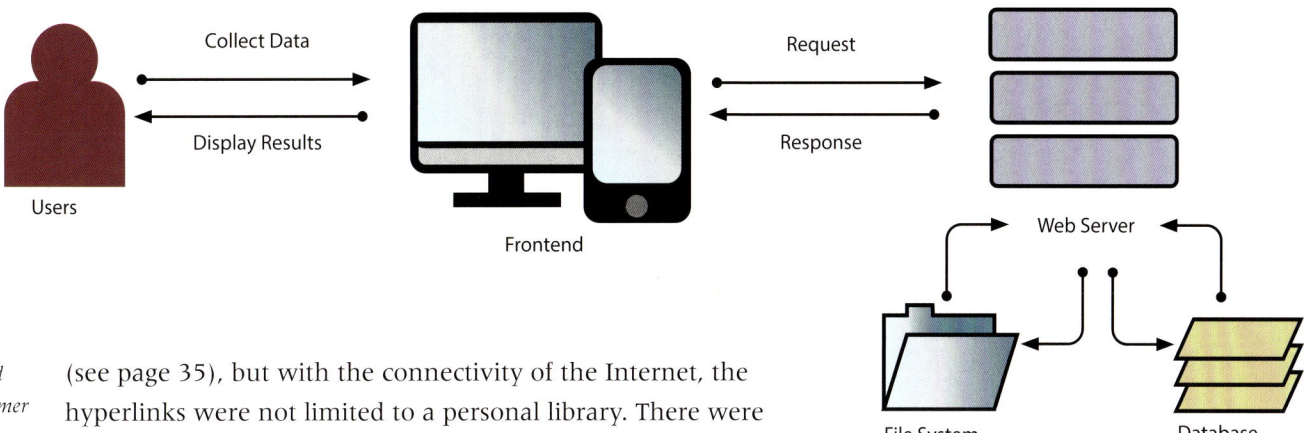

The Web has a frontend and a backend. The former is the interactive display that a user sees. The user makes a request—that could be to read an article or stream a movie—which is directed to the web server where the article or movie is stored. This is the backend. The web server sends back the appropriate response. The backend also maintains a database of information about its users. If they have not paid their subscription, for example, then the response will not be what the user had hoped!

(see page 35), but with the connectivity of the Internet, the hyperlinks were not limited to a personal library. There were already 300,000 computers on the Internet, and a hyperlink could connect with any document made available on any of those devices!

Familiar letters

By October 1990, Berners-Lee had set out the three fundamental technologies that still underpin the system today, which he himself had named the World Wide Web. That term is now shortened to just "Web," but it is still immortalized in the www at the beginning of a web address. Berners-Lee created the address system so every document on the Web would have a unique URL, or Uniform Resource Locator. This address was always preceded by http:// which stands for another of his creations: The HyperText Transfer Protocol. This is the code that facilitates the retrieval of linked resources from across the Web.

By the end of 1990, Berners-Lee's office computer had become the first web server, which hosted documents for the Web—in what came to be called web pages and websites. Berners-Lee realized that his creation would only work if he made it free for everyone. That strategy proved successful. Within ten years, there were 350 million users, and by 2024, two-thirds of all humans (5.5 billion people) used the Web to communicate, socialize, shop, access entertainment, and get news. As well as usurping many traditional industries, the Web also created a new economy that competes for our attention—and we pay for it with our personal data.

HTML

Standing for HyperText Markup Language, this is the simple language created by Berners-Lee for making web pages. At first, these were black and white text documents, but color and pictures were soon to follow. A raw HTML file looks much like a word-processed document, only each element on the page is flanked by codes. These mark how they will be displayed on the web page when it is loaded into the browser. The markups indicate the size and font of the text, its color and position. It is easy enough to grasp—and all the marks disappear when interpreted by the browser. HTML has proved extremely adaptable, although the source files are a lot more complicated today than in the early days. It has been extended to include embedded video and applications, including many processes that run in the background when we look at web pages.

```
<h1>Heading 1</h1>
<b>Bold text</b>
<h2>Heading 2</h2>
<i>Italic text</i>
<a href="url"> Hyperlink </a>
<image src="Image">
```

67 Bluetooth

NAMED FOR A VIKING KING, THIS WIRELESS TECHNOLOGY was created as a link between computing and telephones. It was an early step along the way to taking computing devices off the desk and into everyday life.

Bluetooth is named after Harald Bluetooth, a king of Denmark who had an obvious bad tooth. The logo merges the Norse letters, or runes, for H and B.

As the World Wide Web was being developed to link people and information, Ericsson, a Swedish cellphone manufacturer, was thinking about how to link its products together. The result was Bluetooth—a short-range radio link that was officially launched in 1998 after nine years of development. It is named after a king who unified Denmark. The tech was largely driven by the market for hands-free headsets, with an in-ear speaker and cheek mic. Bluetooth paired this gadget to a telephone handset, so they exchanged data (the components of a voice call) in a secure and seamless way. It all sounds so familiar now, but back then this tech was heartily embraced by the more voluble among us—and those that needed their hands for something else. Bluetooth earpods are the successor gadget today, but the same linking system can unify every bit of tech in your home. From the sound system to the irrigation system, every household appliance can be controlled by a computer—or, more likely, a smartphone (see page 97).

68 GPS Navigation

WE NEED NEVER BE LOST AGAIN. GIVE ME A PHONE WITH BATTERY, and I'll tell you where we are. This truism of modern life is due to the Global Positioning System. Where would we be without it?

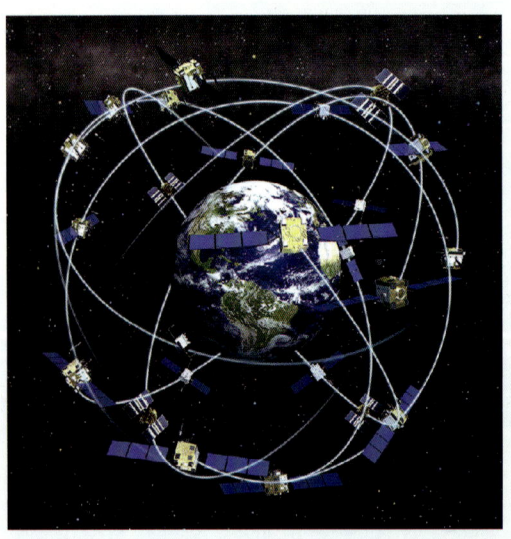

The Global Positioning System (GPS) was the first of four satellite navigation programs. It was originally a U.S. military asset that was built up over the 1980s. It was followed by similar systems launched by Russia, China, and the European Union. In 1991, with the system still being developed, the world's first satellite navigation company, TomTom, started up in the Netherlands. They were way ahead of the pack. GPS went fully live for military purposes in 1995. The public could access a degraded signal in 1996—it gave only a rough estimate of locations—but by 2000, the U.S. government made the full service freely available worldwide. Soon drivers were relying on navigation aids that used GPS to plot a route to a destination. Automation bias, where a person assumes that a computer knows best, began to become evident as drivers

Left: Our mapping apps are relying on signals beaming down from a constellation of satellites that ring the planet. The constellation requires a minimum of 24 satellites, all moving in MEO (medium-earth-orbit) around 12,500 miles (20,000 km) up.

found themselves in parts of the map unsuited to cars, having followed instructions uncritically. In the intervening years, the maps have improved, and extra data is used to enhance route planning. Today's satnavs are sharing their live location—and their speed. When some users find themselves in a jam or slow traffic, drivers traveling behind are offered new routes that divert around the problem.

Mapping

Pedestrians also benefit from the navigation functions in the mapping apps provided on their phones. The most used is Google Maps, which has at least a billion monthly users. The benefits of accurate locations go beyond getting from A to B. Friends and family members are able to share their locations 24 hours a day. They can search the map for services they need, like a particular shop, a park, or a hospital. Knowing where they are means they are always able to find what they need in an unfamiliar area.

However, while sharing a location with a service provider has many benefits, that data can be cross-matched with other information about you and with the location data of the people who will occupy the same spaces as you—by chance or by design. That analysis creates a vivid picture of your day-to-day habits and activities.

Navigation has never been easier. The "automotive navigation system," or satnav, is preloaded with a map. It pinpoints the current location using GPS and then plots a route to the destination. We follow wherever it takes us. The system certainly works, but when it fails we are more lost than ever, because our memories contain a much less detailed mental map of our journeys.

HOW IT WORKS

From just about any point on Earth—unless mountains or buildings get in the way—at least three GPS satellites are overhead at any one time, and can be detected by a unique radio signal. Each signal contains the time it was sent and the location of the satellite. The radio signals travel at the speed of light, but even at that great speed, there is a lag between the time sent and the time received. These tiny lags give the precise distance to each satellite. So once received by a GPS-enabled device—a smartphone's mapping app or a car's satnav, for example—it now knows where the satellites are and how far away they are. This information can be used to calculate the exact position of the device (and you) on the surface of the globe to within a few feet.

69 Virtual Reality

A VIRTUAL REALITY (VR) WORLD IS ONE THAT IS CREATED inside a computer. It dominates the senses and responds to touch and motion. VR is quite old technology, but a VR world that seems real is still quite a futuristic idea.

In 1994, the reality–virtuality continuum was developed as a way of understanding how we might create new computer interfaces where we mix virtual and real environments, the so-called mixed reality. Attempts to convert these ideas into useful applications have so far proven fruitless. Early attempts at VR began in the 1960s using large, cumbersome display systems. By 1989, NASA had developed goggle-like VR headsets that tracked the motion of the head. The tech has largely remained within this platform, and, decades later, the displays are lighter, clearer, and eye-tracking means users can select features by just staring at them. A top-of-the-range headset is the Apple Vision Pro. You can see "through" this using cameras that replay what is in front of you. This illustrates the level of technology that is in use, but even this device has not been a great success. Outside of gaming, VR is not a good match for the real world. That is where users prefer to live and work—so far.

In 2019, the company behind Facebook rebranded as Meta and launched a bold program to create an entirely VR platform called the Metaverse (and sell some headsets in the process). The challenges of visualizing such a world populated by the avatars of unique users proved enormous. After spending $10 billion on the Metaverse, the VR products were quietly sidelined in 2023.

The reality–virtuality continuum, first conceived by Paul Milgrom, illustrates the different kinds of mixed reality. In augmented reality (AR), virtual features, such as text or icons, overlay the real environment, while in augmented virtuality (AV), the VR landscape allows for aspects of the real environment to be displayed as well.

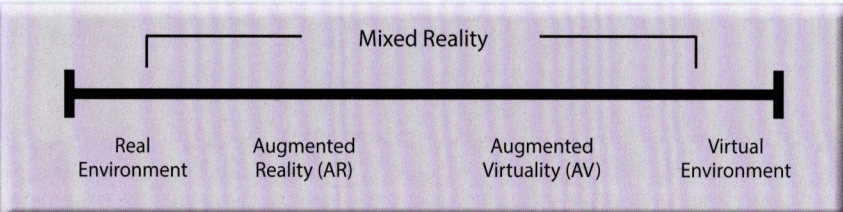

70 E-Commerce

A FIFTH OF ALL PURCHASES ARE NOW MADE ONLINE, and that proportion will only rise further. It's now just called shopping, but more accurately, this area of retail was originally called e-commerce. It all began in 1995.

The Web offered an opportunity to bring people together. It was something new, and those that got involved early were setting up a "home page" as their own little corner of cyberspace. One day we'd all have a home page, perhaps? Others had a more shrewd vision and saw the Web as bringing two types of people together: Customers and retailers.

The start-up

It was always going to be a good idea, and the first person to give it a go was Stephan Schambach, a German who became the first "dot.com" entrepreneur. In 1995, he created Intershop, a software platform that automated the process of shopping. A customer could visit an online store, select a product, and pay for it using this software. Schambach is credited with inventing the online shopping cart, which is a concept that remains intuitively understood.

The advantages of Intershop were obvious: While a real-world store required staff to fulfill their side of the bargain, an online version was able to display the product range on web pages and automate the buying process using a standardized piece of software called a transaction engine. Without a storefront, the physical part of e-commerce was confined to the storeroom or warehouse. Stock levels were maintained by an online database, so customers would only be offered products that were available. The e-commerce model also worked for wholesale. When stock ran low, the system would automatically order more from suppliers. This system enabled a "just-in-time" process, so the warehouse had what it needed, and did not waste space on what it did not need. Artificial intelligence plays an increasing role here (see page 104).

All that remained was for the product to be dispatched and delivered. While e-commerce did away with front-of-store jobs, it has created a boom in warehouse work, with armies of people packing products for delivery. However, that final stage is also increasingly automated with robots. The delivery drivers are still very busy—unless drones and AVs take over that role, too!

E-commerce is used in all traditional areas of retail, from clothing to groceries. However, it has also made it possible for people to sell their own products on a scale too small to support premises in the real world. Additionally, consumers can track and divert their deliveries, make returns easily, and send and receive feedback about the quality of products and services.

71 Chess Computer

IN 1997, A COMPUTER BECAME THE BEST CHESS PLAYER IN THE WORLD. Named Deep Blue, it was an expert system, an early kind of AI that relied on the knowledge of its human programmers.

Deep Blue was created by Big Blue, the nickname for IBM. The system had won the World Computer Chess Championship in 1989, but was beaten by the human champ, the Russian Garry Kasparov. After years of upgrades (and further defeats), there was a rematch in 1997. Of the six games, Kasparov won first and Deep Blue struck back in the second. The next three games were draws.

Deep Blue was a supercomputer loaded with a database of 700,000 top-level chess games. It relied on vast processing power to try out many possible moves, but there were too many to try them all. Instead, Deep Blue used a search algorithm that evaluated the advantage of each move based on the state of the board. It opted for the move with the best odds of leading to a win. In the final game, Kasparov hoped to use this aspect of Deep Blue's game to force it to play too cautiously. The strategy failed, and Kasparov resigned after only 19 moves. Deep Blue was the champion of the world!

Garry Kasparov is one of the most successful chess players in history, staying at the top of the game for longer than anyone else. Deep Blue did not behave as he expected—unlike his human opponents.

72 The Optical Disc

IN THE LATE 1990S, THE MOST USER-FRIENDLY COMPUTER STORAGE was all about little shiny discs that were read with a laser.

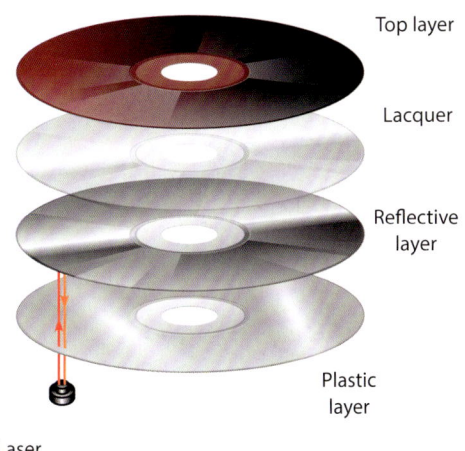

In 1997, a new storage medium was introduced in the United States: The Digital Versatile Disc, or DVD. Its consumers were already familiar with the idea. At first glance, the DVD looked just like a CD, or Compact Disc, which was still the main medium for music in those days. Both are examples of optical discs, but the DVD could store nearly 5 GB, seven times more data than a CD. That made the DVD versatile enough—hence the name—to hold an entire movie or a useful chunk of computer files.

As in all optical discs, the surface has a spiral containing hollows, or pits. Spinning the disc makes a laser run along this spiral, reflecting off the flat surface but not off the pits. The pattern of pits creates a corresponding pattern of flickers in the laser. A detector equates the on-and-off laser reflections as the 1s and 0s of computer code.

Optical discs have several layers. The pits are on the lower plastic layer. Next is a metallic reflective coating, which is protected by a third layer of lacquer. The top layer can be printed—or written—on.

73 E-Ink

THE DEMISE OF PAPER AND THE PRINTED BOOK HAVE LONG BEEN PREDICTED. It's still here (in your hands). However, a 1990s invention has been able to replicate the features of printed matter in electronic form.

An "e-reader" shows any page of any book at any time. However, the displays used by computers are heavy and energy hungry. They also glow, making them hard to look at for long periods of time. Pale paper reflects light, while the dark print does not, a setup that is much easier on the eye. In 1997, a team at MIT began developing e-ink, an electronic display that handled light in the same way. The system uses tiny black and white capsules. These have opposite electrical charges, so are pulled up to the screen or pushed away by creating a pattern of charge that corresponds to text. It took a decade to perfect, but today 40 percent of books are read on e-readers.

The e-ink capsules are floating in transparent spheres, one for each pixel of the display. The screen applies a charge to each pixel, creating a black or white dot. A pixel can also be charged half-and-half, creating a gray mix of black and white.

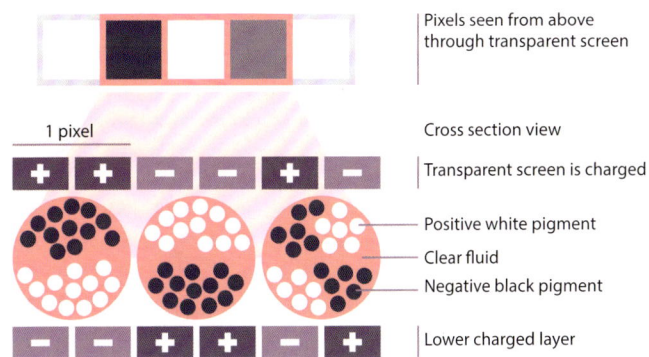

74 Search Engines

WE LIVE IN A DOT.COM WORLD, WHERE THE ADDRESS OF A WEBSITE can be the only thing a customer or user needs to know. In 1998, a company called Google showed everyone what a dot.com could do.

As the World Wide Web grew, it became necessary to search its contents to find the right pages. Early simple search engines were based on keywords, a relatively simple approach, as long as you had every word on the Web indexed. For the first three years of the World Wide Web's existence, its contents was listed by hand. Tim Berners-Lee, the Web's creator, maintained a record of web pages that could be accessed on the primordial web server he hosted at CERN.

Gathering data

In 1993, automated systems took over with software called web crawlers, which created primitive catalogs of file names and titles of every web page. As this name suggests, this software moved steadily through every page of the Web, recording its contents in a searchable database. Any new pages that were added had to wait for the crawler to get back to them. The first all-text search facility—or engine—called WebCrawler, appeared in 1994. However, as the Web grew in size, the time needed to review and update its text contents grew and grew—as did the demand from users to search for something useful and relevant. Into this space sprang several start-up search companies, including Yahoo, Excite, and AltaVista.

At first, these search engines were based on a directory of websites and pages. Later, they began to return results for users' keyword searches based on a page's text contents. Full-text searching like this was a big step, but common search terms of the kind entered by non-technical public users of the Web, who were growing in number, turned up thousands of near-identical pages that all contained those words. The Web was creating a content paradox. There was so much unique information available that it was almost impossible to find what you wanted. In 1998, Larry Page and Sergey Brin, a pair of mathematicians working at Stanford University, developed a method for cutting through all the noise.

The name Google has become a verb. We don't search the Web for something, we google it. As new, more powerful AI search tools are adopted, the world of Internet search is in flux. It remains to be seen whether we carry on googling things and, if we do, whether we use google.com to do it!

GOOGOL

The brand name Google is said to be a misspelling (a serendipitous one, for sure) of the term googol. This is the nonsense name given to the number 10^{100}—a ten followed by 100 zeros. That's a big number—a billion has a mere nine zeros. To add to the fun, the search giant's headquarters is the Googleplex. A googolplex is also a number. This time 10^{googol}, or 10 with a googol of zeros. It is said that paper with a googolplex printed on it would not fit in the known Universe.

10000000000000000000000000000000000000000000000000000000000000000000000000000000000000000000000000000...

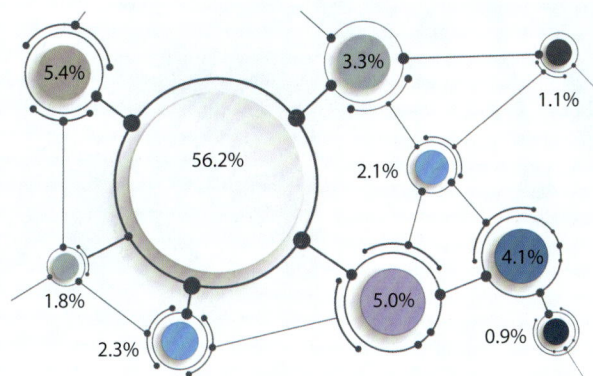

A search engine is able to rank web pages based on their links to other resources on the Web. Each link is assigned a value, or weight, based on its relevance.

Search engines are now able to search for images as well as words.

Ranking system

Page and Brin were the founders of Google. Their business was based on their PageRank algorithm, which was able to rank the list of pages served up by a keyword search into a more useful order—with the best hits at the top. A web page's rank was based on how many other pages were linked to it and how many of them were linked to each other. All these links were given weightings based on other parameters, such as how often a user arrived at a page through links from another. Of the pages that match the search, the one that gets the most traffic is probably the most useful. The reasoning was simple enough, but the mathematics was not. In one sense, Google turns web pages into a vast multidimensional shape, with the sides of the shape being the links. The "shape" of the data is constantly being updated as users click around the Web.

Google helped pave the way for the personalization of search. Your personal history of web use refines the page ranks to meet your unique needs—and of course, that unique data set is how Google makes its revenue. Searching with Google, Bing, or another engine is free at the point of use, but there is a new saying (that's getting old fast): "If you're not paying for the product, you are the product." The search engines use your data to personalize web adverts. Pay attention in math class, folks; Page and Brin are currently the 10th- and 11th-richest people on the planet, respectively!

A MATH COMPANY

Google was founded by mathematicians, and the technology behind Web searches and other services is based on data science, an arm of mathematics. Page and Brin relish their roots in math, so much so that when Google (now reorganized into Alphabet Inc.) was floated on the stock market in 2004, the company issued shares worth $2,718,281,828. Generally, companies value themselves with more rounded numbers. However, mathematicians would see that the Google shares figure was the first ten digits of e, a mathematical constant.

75 Wi-Fi

A CONSEQUENCE OF THE MINIATURIZATION OF COMPUTING WAS THE PROLIFERATION OF DEVICES. They all needed to be connected together and to the Internet, and all those wires running through the home were too limiting. A wireless solution was agreed upon at the close of the 20th century that promised reliable links.

A modern home is a haven for wireless gadgets. Wi-Fi will connect over a range of 30 feet (10 m), although steel elements in a house will impede signals. The radio signals can be relayed into blackspots by a booster. Alternatively, powerline extenders divert the Wi-Fi signals as an AC-current signal through the house's electrical circuits.

The 1990s saw a revolution in wireless telecoms, as cellular telephones set us free to talk and walk, and talk some more. By the end of the decade, demand began to grow for phones to connect to the Web. The content available at the time was limited, but the area of "mobile Internet" was obviously only going to grow. However, cellular connectivity was patchy and expensive. More homes were getting Internet connections, so the prospect appeared of using that for handheld devices.

The obvious answer was a wireless connection that filled the home—but did not interfere with the signals next door! There were many technologies of this kind, based on radio signals being sent and received from a hub, or router, which served as the gateway to the Internet. The difficulty was maintaining contact with each device in the home, with the signals bouncing around off structural features and interfering with each other. The system that eventually solved this issue was developed by Australian astronomers who had aimed originally to create a method of disentangling signals from micro black holes in deep space. In 1999, the industry agreed to a standard protocol for devices of all kinds to use. The system was named Wi-Fi, a name that has lost its edge since. It links the term "wireless" with "hi-fi," which was the high-fidelity music system that many households would have had at the time. The idea was that the rhyming Wi-Fi was a wireless connection that could be relied on.

76 iPod

THIS WAS NOT THE FIRST PERSONAL MUSIC PLAYER, but when it was launched in 2001, it marked a huge change in the way people would consume music—and, one day, all media.

MP3: COMPRESSED MUSIC

The iPod was built on an innovation from the 1980s. This was the creation of the mp3, a file type that compressed digital sound files. Once compressed by this system, a song took up only 8 percent of the original data. The format was created because of how hard it was to share music and other audio through the young Internet. High-quality sound needed 1.4 million bits of information per second.

In 1989, the Fraunhofer Institute in Germany came up with an algorithm to remove the unheard details of sound stored in the code. Everything we heard was still there! This technology fell under the auspices of a global body called the Moving Picture Experts Group, which agreed on industry standards for media. The file type was designated as Audio Layer-3, or mp3.

The market for personal music players was well established. In the 1980s, the Walkman was the go-to tech, playing music on cassette tapes. By the 1990s, tapes were being superseded by CDs, and the Discman was a portable player for those. However, disc players faced competition from various media, each offering better sound and more songs held on a smaller device. That included players that stored music as mp3 files (see box).

If this was the aim of a music player, the iPod wiped out the competition at a stroke. It had a little hard disc inside that could store 5 GB, which added up to 1,000 songs. You had an entire music library in your pocket on a device that was only a little chunkier than a modern smartphone.

Entering the walled garden

The iPod was the latest paradigm-shifting product from Apple's Steve Jobs. Typically it was not just a gadget, but an entire industry. One of the barriers to mp3 players predating the iPod (on top of small storage and bad batteries) was the difficulty in getting mp3 versions of your favorite songs. Jobs had thought of that and had launched iTunes, an application for a personal computer that was part song archive and part music store. iPod owners used iTunes to convert the songs on their CDs into a compressed form for the iPod—an mp3 or another format. iTunes played music through the computer as well, of course. New releases could be downloaded straight to the computer; no physical purchase was needed. So, as well as giving customers a high-quality media player, Apple was also selling them the content to play on it. This was described as Apple's "walled garden," where its customers could be entertained, while users of devices made by other brands were locked out. The iPod is now discontinued, but only after undergoing multiple upgrades where it supported video content, games, and web access via Wi-Fi. If it could have made calls, it would have been a phone—a very smart phone. That was Jobs's next idea.

The early versions of the iPod were controlled with a touch-sensitive wheel. A user circled their thumb around to scroll up and down, and clicked the center to select their next track. The audio was not limited to music. Audiobooks worked very well, and people began to share homemade, low-fi talk shows, a bit like a radio broadcast. In 2004, these files were dubbed "podcasts." There are now 150 million podcast episodes available.

77 Hacktivism

IN 2003, A GROUP OF ONLINE ACTIVISTS MADE THEMSELVES KNOWN. They called themselves Anonymous and declared that they would use hacking techniques to encourage political change. For better or for worse, this kind of activity has proven to be a powerful force.

Anonymous members, known as anons, like to hide their identity by wearing a mask from the 1982 graphic novel V for Vendetta, *about an anarchist revolutionary.*

Hackers have often used their powers to help the underdog. Back in the 1900s, Guglielmo Marconi owned the patent for radio, so no one else was allowed to use the technology. In 1903, he gave a public demonstration of his products. Nevil Maskelyne, a magician who wanted to use radio in his act, took over with a more powerful signal. In protest he tapped out the words "Rats, Rats, Rats" in Morse code. Marconi described him as a "scientific hooligan."

Anonymous would have approved, no doubt. They are a decentralized collective, with groups working independently all over the world. Their normal tactic is to bring down websites run by companies and governments. They do this with a DoS, or denial of service, attack, where they automate so many requests for that site that the system collapses. Members of the group see themselves as online Robin Hoods standing up for the oppressed. Their targets think otherwise, and several members have been convicted of offenses. At best, this kind of hacktivism highlights illegal or immoral activities carried out by states or corporations. It has fallen out of fashion in recent years.

However, hacking has become a powerful tool in interstate conflicts. In 2010, Iran's nuclear facilities were damaged by a computer virus, probably released by Israel. A Russian hacking group called Fancy Bear has been linked to many attacks on foreign governments and media organizations. The world's advanced militaries now regard cyberspace as a theater of conflict alongside land, sea, air, and space.

WIKILEAKS

This media organization was funded by Australian hacker-cum-journalist Julian Assange in 2006. Its aim was to create a safe process for whistleblowers to hand over secret, newsworthy information while staying completely anonymous from WikiLeaks. The system worked in some cases, leading to WikiLeaks breaking stories in what was a changing media landscape. In other cases, WikiLeaks struggled to handle the information it received in a professional way. After avoiding arrest for several years, Assange has now been charged with hacking crimes in the United States. Assange denies this, saying he is protected by journalistic freedoms.

78 Video Calling

SINCE ITS INTRODUCTION IN 2003, THE UTILITY OF VIDEO CALLING was only brought home to us during pandemic of the early 2020s. These calls are now an everyday occurrence for many of us—and an *all-day* one for some.

For many years, making a phone call through a screen, so you could see the other person as you talked, was one of those future technologies that seemed obvious, but was never getting any closer to reality. Telephone companies were trying, of course, but they were impeded by two problems.

Firstly, the amount of information in live video is many orders of magnitude higher than required by a voice call. It was possible, but required dedicated lines with a much greater bandwidth than the copper connections many of us still use. Only the most powerful people—rulers and tycoons—had the resources and will for this kind of connection. Secondly, the voice telephone network began and ended with wired handsets. A video call would require a similarly dedicated device, only this time with a screen and camera. It was all too much for the consumer market.

Then came the Internet. Voice and video could be carried through the Internet—just another set of packets of data, along with emails and web traffic. The computer could function as a phone and video screen. The first widespread VoIP—Voice over Internet Protocol—application was Skype. It was free to use, first for voice and later with video. After a patchy start, this way of communicating has become more practical, as Internet services have increased in speed. A video chat service is provided by all the major web platforms. People chat face-to-face with their cellphones or join hundreds of others on live webinars or video conferences.

> **TELEPRESENCE**
> A video call can be enough to make the right connection, but nothing quite beats being there in person. Telepresence is a technology that puts you somewhere in the middle. It combines video calling technology with a simple robot so a person can be present in a room with others from afar—and without leaving home. Studies show that the people present soon treat the robotic visitor as another person. As robotics technology advances, telepresence will become a more viable service. It can be used for social events in a far-off land or for executives to tour facilities without leaving the office.

At a White House reception for disability rights campaigners, this guest has been able to attend using a telepresence robot without having to leave her home.

79 Social Media

ONCE THE WEB TURNED TEN YEARS OLD, IT BEGAN TO CHANGE. It had been a system to connect people to information, and now it was transforming into a way for people to connect with each other.

The industry described this change in approach as Web 2.0. It grew from the ashes of the "dot.com" bubble, where fortunes had been won and lost by enterprises launched to exploit the explosion of Web users. An over-riding truism of the period was that a dot.com business was not judged by its profitability, but by the number of users it could demonstrate. The making money part would come later. As the funding tide receded in the early 21st century, many web business models were found wanting. Online retail, backed up by extant real-word, or "bricks and mortar," brands had a clear path ahead. Amazon.com was showing how buying certain products, such as

Social media can make anyone a celebrity—or someone two strangers can gossip about. A fan has a parasocial relationship with them—the celebrity feels like a friend, even though they will never meet. This phenomenon is boosted by social media. How that will impact real-world social relationships, especially among the young, is an open question.

books, online, but also other straightforward consumables, had many advantages over going to the store.

Do it yourself

In 2001, the web-based encyclopedia Wikipedia was launched. It was intended as a free source of any and all information in the world—a bold aim that was backed by the fact that the contents of the website was to be entirely created by its users. A "wiki" is the name for a website that can be edited by anyone with a browser. It took years to materialize, but the central concept—that an army of authors and editors would self-regulate Wikipedia's vast archive of content—proved to be a success.

Other web models were based on the same essential idea. Users created the content, but instead of visiting to access information or services, they came to access each other. Readers might recognize this as a rather mechanistic description of social media. There were several attempts to harness this user base, but it was Facebook, launched in 2004, that succeeded. It remains the largest social media platform today. Reorganized as Meta, it owns Facebook, Instagram, and WhatsApp, all means by which users can share their most intimate thoughts and wild assertions with their close social circle and the whole world alike. Facebook, led by Mark Zuckerberg, who, at 23, became the youngest self-made billionaire in history, proved adept at developing ways to make the experience rewarding. Users could receive approval, or likes, from friends and strangers. As the platforms developed, a user's data was processed to suggest new links and new ways to socialize online—and to place highly targeted adverts.

A force for good?

From our location in history, social media—and its huge attention economy—sits at the heart of society. Platforms, which now include the likes of YouTube, X, and TikTok, are endowed with billions of users, and the platforms have become content ecosystems. Our friends are there with us, but we are also consuming news and entertainment, and the algorithms that keep our attention show how to merge those two things together. Human society is glued together by nosiness and gossip, and social media has industrialized it. By design or by accident, it creates a bubble around each of us, where we are exposed to what we like and shielded from what we don't. As such, exposure to disagreeable people or ideas seems especially noxious. Most of us agree that children should be limited in their use of social media. Is this a job for parents or for the state?

MEMES

"All your base are belong to us." That's the first Internet meme. Maybe google it. Meme is derived from "memory" and "gene" and is an idea that spreads itself, changing as it moves from mind to mind, person to person. The Web is good at that kind of thing, and while the initial concept of the meme has faded somewhat, the Internet meme has taken on a new meaning. Memes are pictures (or animations) with text. They are easily created and gently parodic, meant to poke fun. They have become a shorthand way for social media users (or just "people") to express mood or judgment.

80 Data Mining

AS MORE AND MORE OF OUR TIME AND MONEY WAS TRANSFERRED to online activity, the data trail we left became a valuable commodity. Making sense of it all led to growth in an area of computer science called data science.

Social philosophers might note that at the end of the 20th century, the function of information had changed. No longer did we gather information to develop the human project—a process begun in the Renaissance to improve the lot of man through reason and innovation. This is not to say that those endeavors do not continue, and we steadily benefit from them still. However, we also use that information, most notably the personal data of each of us, for other means, and our connected technology means that data is being captured with ever greater speeds. Data scientists, who mix mathematics, statistics and computer science, are employed to mine this data for meaning. For the most part, this means "business intelligence," which analyzes consumers and suppliers to maximize commercial activity.

Data miners will take their data through a series of steps to ensure that any patterns they find contain something meaningful.

Data collection

This approach is not particularly new, but by the mid-2000s, gathering data was becoming an intrinsic part of the shopping process. Online shops asked for reviews on every aspect of the service and product, and bricks-and-mortar businesses offered special deals for those who signed up to loyalty schemes that tracked purchasing habits. So what does it all mean?

Data mining works best if the information is neatly labeled, so it is completely clear how all the values relate to one another—things like prices, ages, and locations. Retailers collect this structured data easily enough, and the inferences drawn from it have some veracity. For example, customers who buy beer also buy pop tarts. However, data miners are also working with unstructured data sets. There are relationships in there, but the data must be refined to find meaningful ones. That is not always the result. During the COVID-19 pandemic, data mining was used to create diagnostic tests from chest scans. Sick people were scanned lying down; healthy people were standing. The system just diagnosed whoever was scanned lying down with the virus!.

81 Smartphone

WHAT DO YOU GET IF YOU CROSS A TELEPHONE WITH A COMPUTER?
A smartphone! This is not a joke. Today, two-thirds of all computing is done using these handheld devices that fit in your pocket.

A smartphone is an easy sell. They bring all aspects of online life into the palm of the hand. You can more or less work, rest, and play all with this one device. The era of the smartphone begins in 2007 with the iPhone from Apple. This was the next step in Steve Jobs's vision to revolutionize consumer tech. However, others had already tried it out. The first attempt was the Simon Personal Communicator, which was launched in 1993. This 18-ounce (510-gram) handheld cell phone and personal digital assistant featured a touchscreen with icons you could tap with a stylus. As well as being able to make phone calls, it could send and receive emails and faxes. It also had an address book, a calendar, and calculator. Early adopters of the technology liked the way it combined all this into one gadget, but with its limited list of functions, it remained a business tool. By the 2000s, the Blackberry, with its neat screen and tiny keyboard, was easier to use, but was still largely focused on business.

By the time the iPhone arrived, even entry-level cellphones already had games and cameras, and had limited Internet access. The iPhone completely re-imagined the device. In so doing, the phone application was just one of many available. The basics, like email, a calendar, and a music player, came preloaded, but building on the iTunes platform, iPhone users could buy all kinds of apps for whatever they wanted to do. The other chief innovation lay in the interface, which combined the screen and the control. Apps were graphical icons that were launched by touch, and the keyboard had "soft keys" on the screen along with the text being written.

Today, there are 7 billion smartphone users. Mostly, it is young children that don't have one. Half of Americans admit to being "addicted" to theirs, meaning it takes up their attention more than they might like. Phones now come with screen-time controls. Do you use them?

The first iPhone was small by today's standards. As with any product line, the next generation of smartphones must be an improvement on the last. The big changes were screen size and battery life. A bigger battery means a bigger phone, and so an equilibrium has now been reached with phones being about 6 inches (15 cm) long. The battle for customers is now fought with upgrades in camera quality and AI-powered photo manipulation.

ANDROID
Around 80 percent of smartphones today run a version of the Android operating system, which is based on Linux and owned by Google. It's licensed to phone manufacturers (other than Apple), who will customize it for their products. However, the distribution and sale of apps are controlled through Play Store, Google's "walled garden" (see page 91).

82 Gig Economy

As we have seen, the Internet brings people together. It can make connections that would be almost impossible in the real world. In the late 2000s, that ability was converted into a whole new type of work.

It is estimated that around half a billion people are working in the gig economy, using apps to find work and be given tasks.

Statisticians talk about long tails of data. They refer to the extreme ends of a distribution containing very few data points. In the real world, people of tall and small stature occupy long tails. They struggle to find clothes and shoes that fit. They are few and far between, and it is not cost effective for high-street retailers to carry stock for them. There are specialist producers to meet those needs, but all of us fit into a long tail somewhere. Perhaps you collect something obscure or need a spare part for a discontinued appliance. The Internet has come to the rescue. While eBay led the way, there are now many online services where niche demands are met by niche suppliers. The website is just an agent that is paid for making the introductions.

In 2008, this agency model found another outlet with Airbnb, a service for renting out spare rooms and empty apartments. All the admin is handled through an app. In 2009, Uber followed, with drivers offering rides to passengers. A smartphone app locates the pickup, takes the money, plans the route (and harvests the data). This is the gig economy, where service providers are paid piece-rate for one-off jobs, or gigs. The sector has ballooned. There are apps for deliveries of take-out food, odd jobs, and tutoring. The apps work, but employment experts push back that the lack of workplace protections is one way the agency model reduces costs and beats its competition.

83 Wearables

WHAT'S NEXT FOR CONSUMER TECHNOLOGY? Now that there is a smartphone in almost everyone's pocket or purse, there are opportunities for smaller peripherals to be worn about the person. This is wearable technology.

What was the first wearable technology? It is a toss-up between VR goggles and headphones. VR headsets are not necessarily designed for wearing out and about. Apple's Vision Pro headgear can be, but that doesn't mean anyone does it. Have you? Meanwhile, a lot of people use headphones or earpods, wirelessly connected by Bluetooth, of course. However, "wearables" form a different category. They are worn on the wrist like a watch—they may be an actual watch, a smartwatch—or as rings. They can even be stuck to the skin or implanted under it.

Wearables are mostly designed to have appeal as accessories, but their primary function is to collect data about the wearer's body. At its simplest, that might be a step counter, like the Fitbit wristband, one of the first mass-market wearables, which launched in 2009. The devices may also measure body temperature and heart rate by shining a light on the skin (on the wrist generally) to monitor blood flow beneath. It documents sleep patterns by recording the movement of the body as we relax and fidget our way through the sleep cycle. Via an app, this data is used to create an overall analysis of physical activity levels and general health. Health applications are a key driver, but wearables can also handle messaging and payments. Wearable technology represents a significant change in the way we interact with technology.

A smartwatch used for fitness training combines the weight, age, and sex of the wearer to generate a record of health indicators and athletic performance.

84 Cryptocurrency

INVESTORS AND TECH ENTREPRENEURS like to talk about disruptive technology, something that gives a business advantage. There is perhaps nothing more disruptive than Bitcoin, which has re-imagined money itself!

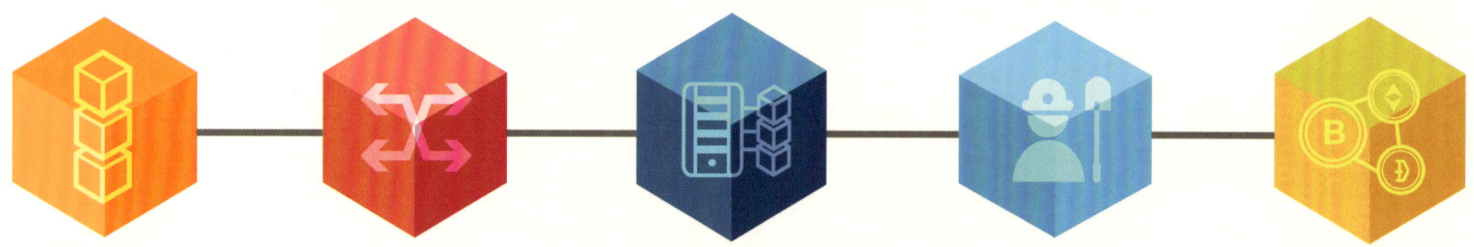

Bitcoin is not real. It's all just code inside a computer. One could argue that other forms of money lack authenticity in other ways. So, in the end, if someone wants a Bitcoin, it has a value. A person's Bitcoin wallet is secured by a long passcode. If that gets lost, so do the Bitcoins!

First things first, Bitcoin and other cryptocurrencies are not really currencies at all. A currency, like the U.S. dollar, is backed by a government. That ultimately has value because we all agree that it does. Crypto is a kind of commodity money. It has value because it is ultimately linked to a finite resource, and the more scarce that resource, the more value the money has. Either way, dollars and Bitcoins have value, and you can use them to buy things. The dollar, like all currencies, is controlled by a government that can act to influence its value. They can issue more of it, for example. Bitcoin and other cryptocurrencies are not controlled by anyone, and one day they will run out, or rather, one day there won't be any more of them. In the meantime, however, the value of Bitcoin makes it something a lot of people want. So what is it?

Maintaining trust

Cryptocurrency exists solely as virtual "coins" recorded on a computer somewhere. When it is spent, the system alters the record of who owns the coin now. The crypto part relates to how the record, or ledger, of who owns what is stored away—behind unbreakable code. This is required to ensure that the ledger remains immune from attack and will always be a credible record of ownership. If people ever began to mistrust the system then the it would immediately lose any value. The first cryptocurrency was Bitcoin, which launched in 2009. There are other systems, including Ethereum, which issues coins called Ether. The systems share some similarities, and both remain trusted. There have been some large-scale thefts and losses of coins, but not due to the underlying system.

Getting to work

Both coins have to be earned through hard labor—not physical work, but computer work. The people who work for coins are called miners. Miners devote their computer resources to solving very complicated and long-winded math calculations. Once the calculation is completed, the miner earns a coin. The work being done is not for the sake of it. The miners' computers are maintaining the ledger of ownership, known as the blockchain. As previously discussed, this is the master record of all the world's coins and all the transactions.

Bitcoins are mined in blocks, and the first one, the "Genesis Block," was created on January 3, 2009. This was done by Bitcoin's creator, Satoshi Nakamoto. Nakamoto has never revealed who he is. He may be a cipher for a team of developers. It's a mystery! The first block had 50 coins in it. Every ten minutes since then, a new block has been added with the details of the next set of coins. After every 210,000 coins, the number of coins per block is halved.

To date, more than 19 million Bitcoins have been mined, and there are now 6.25 coins per block. The work needed to mine a block has not changed, so the reward in coins is steadily dropping. However, at the same time, the value of each coin is rising, because they are becoming harder to make. When the number of coins reaches 21 million, the number of coins per block will have reached zero. This is not going to happen all that soon—the current estimate is the year 2140—because blocks will start to contain smaller and smaller fractions of coins, known as satoshi. There are 100 million satoshi in a Bitcoin, and at the time of writing, 10,000 satoshi are worth $6.40. Miners must think that by the time they are working for satoshi, the value will have gone up!

WIDELY DISTRIBUTED

The blockchain is not stored in one place. If it was in one place it would be more vulnerable to attack. Instead, it is stored on a distributed network that links the mining computers. The information stored on one of these computers is useless without all the other bits. Hackers would have to attack all the computers at once, which is impossible. A distributed network has no central node or any hubs at all. It is more secure than other forms of network.

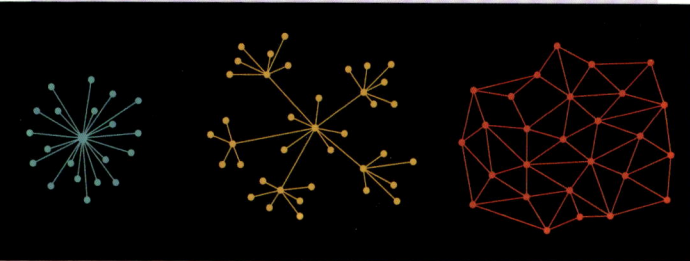

Centralized   Decentralized   Distributed

ENVIRONMENTAL DAMAGE

Cryptocurrency mining—especially for Bitcoin—is staggering in its energy use and carbon footprint. Miners assemble large numbers of powerful processors originally designed for creating graphics (and now also used to accelerate machine learning). All that computing power uses up 0.75 percent of all the electrical power in the world! That is more than the energy used by Argentina or Australia. Some miners even have their own coal and gas-fired power plants!

A lot at stake

The mining process for maintaining the Bitcoin blockchain uses a system called proof of work. The miners are in competition to complete a task and earn the coins, and that work may be fruitless—and is very wasteful (see box, left). The Ethereum currency uses a proof of stake, whereby a miner is nominated as the single validator of a block, so others do not waste their effort and resources.

85 Watson, the Quiz AI

BUOYED BY THE SUCCESS OF DEEP MIND, IBM WAS KEEN to show what more it could do with artificial intelligence. In 2011, it made another astounding success.

The next IBM AI project was called Watson, after the company's first CEO, Thomas J. Watson. Instead of tackling a single big problem like chess, Watson was built to tackle any problem you gave it! That said, it was limited to problems posed in a certain way, but as long as the solution was based in fact, Watson would find it. In doing so, Watson was an early example of how machine learning could enhance AI (see page 104). In 2011, Watson shocked the world by appearing in a special episode of the long-running U.S. game show *Jeopardy!*. It competed against two champions, Brad Rutter and Ken Jennings. The show's gimmick is to give a statement of fact as a clue, and the contestants score points by posing the right question. Watson used a system called a language model to understand clues, and then highly efficient search algorithms to find the answer. And it did all this in under three seconds. Needless to say Watson won its appearance on *Jeopardy!*.

IBM Watson is still at work, getting ever more refined. Its natural language processor was used to create CIMON, an AI assistant for use on the International Space Station. The AI was also asked to unjumble the mix of data collected from cancer patients to find better treatments and diagnostic signals. However, to date the AI has not proven to be more effective at it than human experts.

86 Cloud Computing

WHEN YOU STORE YOUR PHOTOS IN "THE CLOUD" where do they go? Don't look up. The cloud is found in vast data centers all around the world.

The term "cloud computing" dates back to an internal memo from 1996 at Compaq, a large hardware manufacturer. However, the core of the idea can be traced to the thinking of John McCarthy, a computer scientist who was there at the very beginning of the field. He was a student of John von Neumann and was present at the Dartmouth Workshop in 1956, where the first foundations of AI computing were laid (see page 42). In 1961, while a research fellow at MIT, McCarthy suggested that computing resources could be sold as a utility, like the way water and electricity are sold. The customer would be billed for how many computing resources they consume. Back then, this was not quite as radical an idea as it might seem. By "computing," McCarthy

VPN

A VPN is a "virtual private network." It is a service built to hide the location of your device (and you). It can also "spoof" a location to give the impression that you are somewhere else in the world, which has its uses. The VPN does this by connecting you to the Internet via a private network rather than a public one, like a cell tower or your Internet service provider (ISP). The VPN encrypts all the traffic before it gets to the Internet. Anyone tracking your traffic has nothing to go on. In many countries your ISP has to, by law, keep a record of what you do online. A VPN protects your communications and creates a further barrier for hackers (who use them as well, of course).

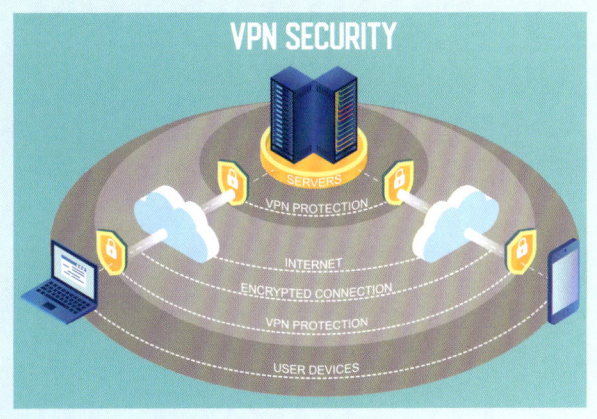

was referring to the use of a mainframe. In those days, mainframes operated on a system called remote job entry, where users would submit jobs to be run by technicians on a mainframe somewhere else.

There were obvious disadvantages with this, so the industry moved to distributed computing, where many computers are networked together so they can share their resources. This worked better, but was limited by the hardware available. In the early 2000s, cloud computing appeared as a hybrid approach, where storage and processors could be used on-demand. The hardware could be anywhere, but high-speed Internet made the location irrelevant.

Tech companies like Amazon realized they had spare computing capacity for much of the time, and so made it available for other enterprises as a billed utility. Cloud computing is now something available to all. Microsoft started OneDrive back in 2007, and Apple's iCloud and Google's Drive followed. These cloud services offer storage, along with a suite of applications, hosted in the cloud. Just log in on any device, and you are ready to go!

Everyday consumers mostly use the cloud to store photos, videos, and backups for their devices. However, it is also useful for storing work documents to share with others or access from multiple devices.

87 Machine Learning

After decades of slow progress and false starts, it became clear that advances in AI required a system that could be trained, essentially creating its own algorithm. This system is machine learning.

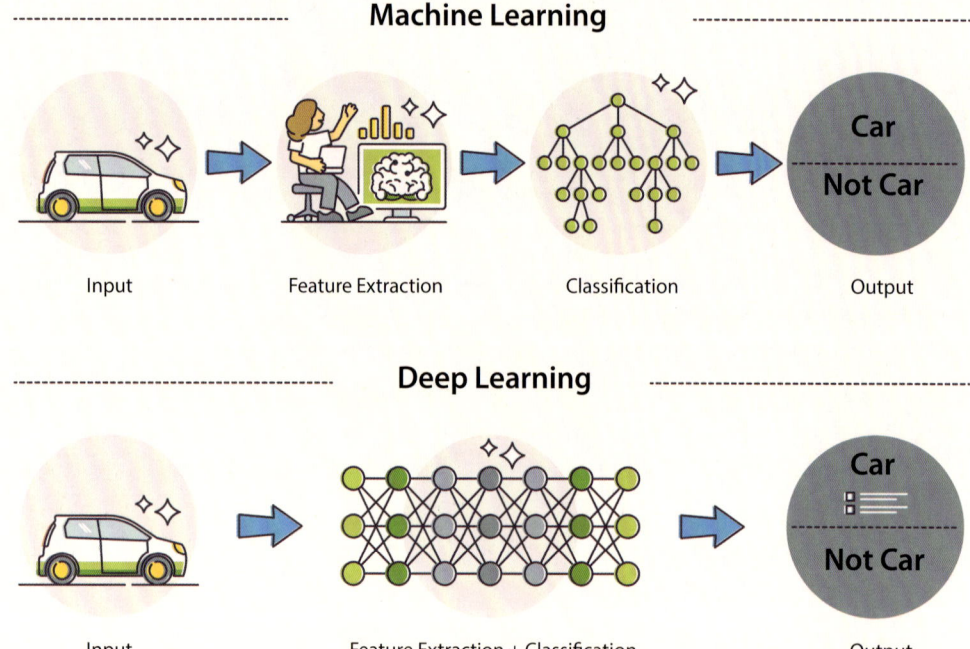

Machine learning is the system behind narrow AIs, like those controlling a car's autopilot. Deep learning is one technique that is proving to be very effective at making sense of the world without too much human intervention.

Machine learning is the catch-all term for a number of techniques. They are often used together to create an AI that is able to interpret data, extract the appropriate meaning from it, and give an appropriate response to it. The techniques range from statistical analysis and logical reasoning to decision trees (see box, opposite) and deep learning. The latter is the poster child of machine learning, because it is deep learning that has led to the recent highly publicized advances in generative AI (see page 116).

Machine learning relies on there being a relationship between the input data and the outputs. So once an AI is fully trained by machine learning, it will be able to identify the correct output just from the input. The normal example given here is recognizing pictures of cats. However, machine learning is also deciding whether a bank customer is a credit risk, or figuring out what products to stock in a store or warehouse by region and time of year. Machine learning is also creating AIs that can diagnose disease from scans and test data, and then suggest the best treatments for that case.

Patterns in the data

The AI has the ability to recognize appropriate outputs from inputs alone, because it has been trained by machine learning. During the training phase, the machine learning model, built by computer scientists, is given a big data set of both input and output. It then learns ways to link the two together. The best example of this is deep learning.

Deep learning uses an artificial neural network (ANN) built up of perceptrons (see page 53). These are devices (physical or virtual) that classify inputs into one of two outputs. This copies the way simple brain cells work, hence why they form an ANN. The ANN has many layers, one receiving inputs and the other giving outputs, and several "hidden" layers in between. Each perceptron, or node, is connected to all the others in the neighboring layer. So for an AI being trained to spot cats in pictures, the first layer might be looking for data patterns that indicate the shape of a cat's body. A weighting is assigned to that input to indicate how likely it is that this input shows a cat's body. The input data moves to the next node according to that weighting. In the following layers, the data might be classified according to the shape of the eyes, nose, or fur patterns. The ANN then outputs whether it classifies the picture data input to show a cat or not—with some degree of certainty.

DECISION TREE

This method is often used in supervised machine learning, where the data is very clear and well understood. It classifies data like deep learning does, but in an easier and faster way. The tree has nodes that ask questions about the data, and the answers lead to one of the connected nodes. This process happens many times over, until the data arrives at a final "leaf" node. The highly simplified example below is a decision tree for working out if it is a good time for a round of golf.

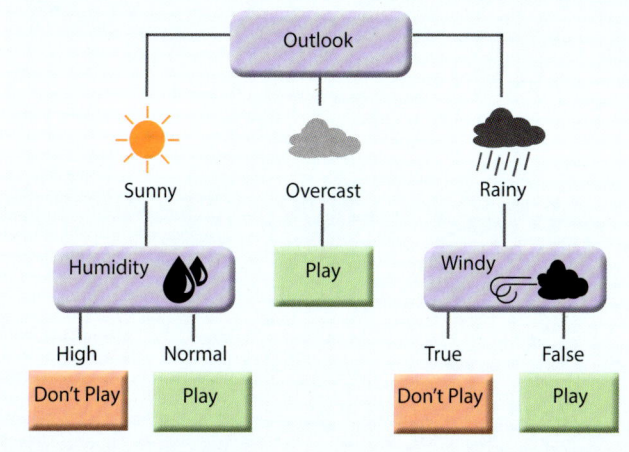

The ANN can do this, because it is trained by trial and error. Inputs pass through the layers at random, generating an output and its score of certainty. This is then compared against the actual output in the training data to create an error score. The data is then sent back the other way through the ANN with its error score, in a process called backpropagation . The error score is used to figure out how much each node in each layer contributed to the error, and they are tweaked accordingly. It will do a better job with the next data input. This back-and-forth process is run millions of times, and in the end the ANN will spot cats more accurately than you!

Learning types

Machine learning falls into two broad camps: Supervised and unsupervised. Supervised learning is simpler, because it uses training data that is already well organized. Unsupervised learning makes use of data that is disorganized, as is much of the data captured from the real world. It may not be difficult for a person to label this data correctly, but it would take a long time. Unsupervised learning does this job all by itself!

FUZZY LOGIC

Sometimes following a binary logic of true–false, stop–start, or on–off, is not the best way to interpret the world and interact with it. The world—or at least the data we collect about it—is fuzzy. This is why the Iranian-American computer scientist Lotfi Zadeh created fuzzy logic. He reasoned: "The classes of objects encountered in the real world do not have precisely defined criteria of membership." In a complex system, classifying data into one set of things or another does not give the best description of the system. Fuzzy logic is a way that data can belong to two (or more) sets at once. For example, weather can be cloudy, sunny, and rainy even, each to a varying degree. So the weather conditions at a location would fit into all three sets, or classes, of weather, each with a fractional membership value. When the clouds clear and the sky goes blue, the weather conditions have "unfuzzed." It's only sunshine here!

88 Biometrics

IN 2013, THE FIRST MASS-MARKET SMARTPHONES WERE LAUNCHED that could be unlocked by a unique fingerprint, rather than a secret code. Biometrics, or using the body for identification, is now an everyday occurrence.

It is true what our parents say. We are all very special. We all have a unique set of physical features that will stay constant even as we age. From about the age of 12, our face shape is built on a fixed pattern of features, such as the distances between the eyes and chin to forehead. These will stay in proportion even as you grow and age. Similarly, our fingerprints are unique, as is the sound of our voices. So as long as these features are captured in enough detail, they can be a fail-safe form of ID. Today, smartphones scan the user's face as well as their thumbs, while almost all countries issue passports with biometric data on an embedded chip.

Biometrics works by comparison. The raw data is collected by scanning a finger or face—or a photo. This data is stored as a graph or network of connected points. The next scan is compared against this master copy. If it is near enough, then the phone unlocks, the e-gate at the airport opens, or the bank transfer is approved. The comparison is made using an algorithm created by machine learning. For authenticating a person's identity with the data stored in a device or document, the system works well. However, the same technology can be deployed to look for a face in the crowd, scanning hundreds of faces to find one. It is very likely to find several people that *might* be the target, and due to biases in the training data, the faces of minority people are currently more likely to be the victims of mistaken identity.

When facial recognition scans the face, it converts it into a network of simpler shapes. To unlock your phone, the system is looking for some basic features in the face.

89 Near-Field Technology

CASH HAS BEEN AROUND FOR MORE THAN 2,700 YEARS, but its days might be numbered. Contactless payments use a tiny, short-range radio link to perform a transaction. Why bother with coins and bills?

With near-field technology, no cash is required—and in some stores not accepted, either. There are valid concerns with this method of payment. It requires an expensive phone and full bank account, so it disenfranchises people who cannot access these things.

By 2014, paying small amounts of money without ever needing cash had become widespread. Simply tapping a bank card on the card reader was enough. Even if you'd forgotten your wallet, all the necessary details could be stored on your phone, making it a virtual wallet. The same kind of contactless technology used in the card allows the smartphone to transmit the necessary financial details. This innovation is called near-field technology.

Obviously a bank card has no battery, so how does it work? The card has a coiled antenna inside, which becomes electrified when a powerful radio source is close enough—a few inches at most. Once electrified, the tag sends out a unique radio signal, which is picked up by the card reader. That is enough to prove the identity and bank details of the payer, at least for small sums. Smartphone payment apps work in the same way and can be used for larger payments, because they require the payer to have identified themselves using biometrics.

90 Smart Speakers

HELLO THERE! WHAT'S A SMART SPEAKER? This is a question that's had a valid answer since around 2014. This was when Amazon's Echo was launched, and people started conversing with their devices in earnest.

It is predicted that three-quarters of U.S. homes will have a smart speaker by the 2030s. Apple, Google, and many others now offer them. The term "smart" is a hard-working word that embraces the notion of an inanimate object doing at least some of the thinking for us. As its name suggests, a smart speaker is an audio device, primarily used to play the radio or music. But you can ask it questions—and it talks back. All the work is happening in the cloud—or in a data center far away. Just as IBM Watson did (see page 102), your voice is converted into a keyword search that results in your latest favorite track, the weather outlook, or some arcane factoid to settle an argument. Its AI is being improved all the time, but, just as we simplify our speech when talking to children, we modify what we say to smart speakers to get the results we want.

91 Haptics

WE FEEL THE WORLD WITH OUR SKIN, just as much as we see and hear it. Haptics is the technology that uses touch as another interface between humans and computers.

Until you pop on a headset and enter virtual reality (VR), we generally underestimate the amount of information we are receiving about the world through our skin. It is telling us about temperature, body position, and gives us touch, of course. Haptic tech recreates the sense of touch by pushing and pulling on the skin, even though there are no physical objects there. Gloves are the most common haptic device, but the same technique can be extended to a full-body suit. Motion sensors are used to track the motion of the hand or body in space. If an avatar meets an object in VR, the haptic tech creates touch feedback on the real body. The sense of touch can be stimulated with puffs of air or beams of ultrasound. The suit can also be fitted with mechanical devices that vibrate or tap the skin to emulate a touch or texture. Mechanical haptics like this are increasingly used for notifications on smart watches and other wearable tech.

Haptic gloves and suits make the experience of virtual reality more immersive. You can feel the VR world and interact with it.

92 The DARPA Robotics Challenge

IN 2015, THE WORLD'S TOP ROBOTIC ENGINEERS TOOK PART IN a competition to build the most capable robots the world had ever seen.

The Defense Advanced Research Projects Agency (DARPA) has a track record of innovation. Known back then as ARPA (see page 59), it was this U.S. agency that, in the 1960s, sowed the seeds that would grow into the Internet, and then the World Wide Web. It also had a hand in satellites, GPS navigation, and autonomous drones. After all, DARPA's purpose is to push the boundaries of innovation, and so in 2012, it launched the DARPA Robotics Challenge (DRC). This competition, culminating in a trial of robots in 2015, aimed at developing semi-autonomous ground robots. These robots were not your basic sci-fi humanoid butlers. Their aim was to be more like a superhero, capable of going into a shattered disaster zone and carrying out complex tasks in conditions too perilous for humans to venture.

EXOSKELETONS

Robotics is not just about making autonomous machines. The same engineering can be used to create powered "mech suits," or exoskeletons. An exoskeleton (right) is a wearable machine that augments the physical abilities of a human operator. It can be used to offer superhuman strength, turning one person into a heavy-lifting machine. An alternative use is to replace body functions, such as helping a paralyzed person walk again. The first exoskeleton, called Hardiman, was produced by General Electric in 1969. Unfortunately, only one arm worked as planned. The machine juddered violently when the full frame was powered up, and it was never used with a person inside. Today, more successful prototypes are being developed for use by infantry soldiers to aid with mobility, and there are even plans for mech suit wrestling!

With that said, the tasks set for the robots were all too human: The robots were asked to drive a utility vehicle (a fire truck seems like the best option) to the site. Then, they had to make their way over a field of rubble, clear debris from a doorway, open a door, and enter a building. Inside, the robot had to climb a ladder and walk along a suspended walkway. Next, it had to smash its way through a concrete panel—it had the tools to hand—to find the valve for a leaking pipe and shut it off. Finally, the robot was asked to connect a fire hose and turn on the water.

Initially, the challenge involved creating computer models of robot types that were tried out in a virtual testbed. In 2015, final trials were held in California, with 23 teams making it to the end. The fastest was Hubo, a robot developed by a South Korean team. Hubo could walk on two legs, but also dropped to its knees and rolled on wheels. It completed the trial in 44 minutes! Several other teams used ATLAS, a humanoid robot built by Boston Dynamics (a robot company created by MIT), specifically for the Robotics Challenge. The MIT team took 50 minutes to finish the trial. Other teams relied on four-legged robots. The robots in the challenge were an example of supervised autonomy, where a human controller can interpret the scene and direct tasks, but the robot does the rest. Autonomous robots would require planning and predictive abilities, which is now the subject of generative AI research (see page 116).

Spot is a four-legged robot from Boston Dynamics. It is used as an autonomous patrol dog in remote locations. It can be fitted with sensors to monitor the activity of machinery, gather data, and look for faults.

93 Data Protection

IN 2016, DIVISIONS BEGAN TO APPEAR ON THE INTERNET. Depending on where you lived—and where your data was stored—different rules applied to what people could do with information gathered about you.

In Europe, most countries use the 2016 rules called General Data Protection Regulations (GDPR). The rules are simple: Personal information is kept safe, it must be accurate, and it only records the minimum necessary to meet the needs of the relationship. If there is no relationship, the data is deleted. In practice, of course, it is more complicated, but the framework gives individuals a path to taking control of their data. California and some other U.S. states have enacted similar controls, but in other places the balance between business, state, and private individuals is very different. When GDPR was launched, the center of the tech world was California. Today, the industry is spreading to other territories, where personal data does not have the same protection. These differences are likely to cause conflict until a global protection system is agreed upon.

94 Quantum Computing

CLASSICAL COMPUTING RUNS ON BINARY SWITCHES. They are either on or off. However, in the quantum realm, it is possible to be both on and off at the same time. What does that mean for computing?

A classical computer system works with bits. Generally speaking, a modern device handles data chunks of 64 bits in one go. That means somewhere on the processor, there are 64 logical circuits that, in that instant, are switched on and off to represent 64 binary digits (1s or 0s) in a particular order. Now imagine a processor that has quantum bits, or qubits. And to help with that, we will just think about 8-bit processors from now on—otherwise the numbers will get ridiculously large, fast. In ways that we'll see later, a quantum bit uses the phenomenon of superposition to be both on and off, 1 and 0, at the same time. According to quantum physics, the features of quantum objects, such as atoms and electrons, are defined by probability, so there is a chance that the qubit represents 1, and there is a chance that it is a 0. What difference does that make?

The information stored on a quantum processor is exponentially greater than on a classical one. One qubit holds two bits of information all by itself. Two qubits hold 4 bits (2^2)

P≠NP
Mathematicians divide math problems into two groups, P and NP. P problems can be solved given enough time. NP problems do have answers, but it would take a supercomputer a near-infinite amount of time to find them. Some NP problems will be just as difficult for quantum computers as classical ones, but there is an overlapping subgroup of problems called "NP-hard" that might be unlocked by quantum computing.

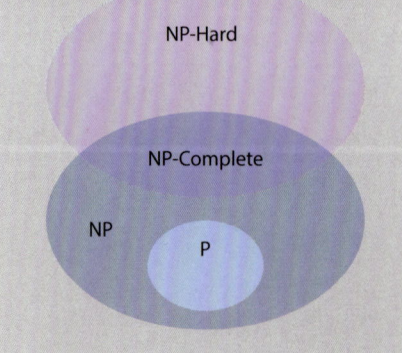

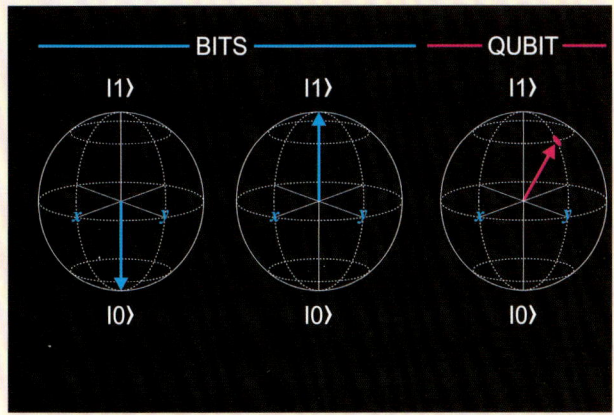

This diagram shows the essential difference between a bit and a qubit. The bit has two states, while the qubit has an infinite number of possible states, as defined by quantum mechanics, the mathematics of quantum physics.

of information, 8 qubits can store 256 bits (2^8). Put another way, an 8-bit classical processor can store any number from 0 to 255. That is the highest possible binary number written with 8 digits. An 8-qubit processor can represent any number from 0 to 115792089237316195423570985008687907853269984665640564039457584007913129639936!

Quantum hardware

With all this said, building a quantum processor is not that easy. There are different designs of quantum bits. One is the ion trap, which is a metal atom with an electron removed, making it an ion. The position of a second electron still attached to the ion is controlled by pulses of laser light. Another qubit system uses loops of superconducting wires. The flow of electricity through them is a quantum behavior. The most promising qubit is a silicon quantum dot, where a single electron is held in a crystal of silicon and controlled by electrical effects. For qubits to function as a processor, they need to be strung together into a unit using another phenomenon called entanglement. This is a spooky feature whereby a change in one qubit results in a simultaneous opposite change in an entangled partner. Instead of emulating a silicon microchip with its registers and cores, quantum processors are long chains of qubits—the current record is 1,000 connected at once. No one expects quantum computers to replace classical ones (we won't have quantum smartphones), but quantum computers could accelerate AI, revolutionize computer modelling, and solve some of the toughest math problems.

Quantum computers look very different from classical ones. To work, they must be isolated from any interference. They work in a vacuum that is kept very cold and is shielded from light, radio waves, and magnetism, all of which would disrupt the quantum states of the qubits.

95 Big Data

THE AMOUNT OF INFORMATION STORED ON THE WORLD'S COMPUTERS is increasing by about 50 percent year-on-year. All that data offers new opportunities to understand the world in a field called Big Data.

The challenge of analyzing Big Data is clustering the vast amounts of data into meaningful classes.

In 2010, there were two zetabytes (ZB, 2,000 billion-billion bytes) stored in computer memory. By 2020 there were 64 ZB, and it will be beyond 200 ZB by the start of the 2030s. Big Data is a natural consequence of the information revolution. The data exists for many different reasons—or for no reason at all. The question is, can we make sense of it? The first problem is that there is so much of it, and it's still growing, fast. Secondly, it is very unstructured. As a result, sets of Big Data have a low information density when compared to regular data collected for a deliberate purpose. However, Big Data works well with inductive statistics, similar to those used in machine learning, that infer general conclusions from relationships discovered in the data.

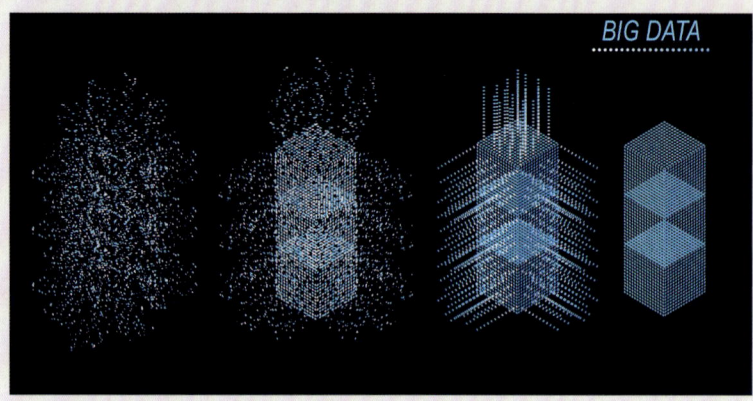

96 Internet of Things

IT MIGHT SEEM STRANGE, BUT THE EARLY INTERNET WAS ALL ABOUT PEOPLE. The network was to connect us to each other and to our machines. Today, people on the Net are a minority of end users. It's all about things.

About two-thirds of all people are Internet users, and that proportion rises if we discount the very young. All you need is a smartphone with service. However, there are already more things connected to the Internet than there are people. At last count, there were just over 8 billion people, and just under 17 billion things on the Internet. The number of human users will rise some more, but the real growth area is in things. By 2030, their numbers will have more or less doubled.

So what is a "thing?" It is any device that collects data and shares it through the Internet. The obvious place to look is in the home, where smart devices are becoming more common. For starters, there are smart speakers, but the list is long and growing. There are smart meters for water and energy use; smart controllers allow us to adjust lighting, heating, and air conditioning from a smartphone app—even far from home.

The cameras of smart security systems transmit images to any screen with authentic logins, and a home owner can see and talk to delivery people through their doorbell. There are even refrigerators, ovens, and toilets with smart features connected via apps. Outside of the home, wearable technology, like a fitness tracker or smart watch, your phone, and maybe your car are also "things" sharing location and usage data when you are out and about. And in the wider world, there are cameras and sensors of all kinds collecting data on traffic jams, weather observations, ocean currents, deforestation, and the production in factories and on farms. Satellites orbiting space are also things on the Internet of Things (IoT). So what's all the fuss about?

Smart living
The IoT is a key driver of Big Data, and all that information being gathered could be used to train AI to take on more of a role in controlling the home, and civic infrastructure as a whole. A smart home would learn to run itself in accordance with your needs, stocking up on foods, maintaining comfort, and checking the toilet for indicators of illness! More widely, power usage from the IoT data could train AIs to run power grids in a more efficient way, and reducing the need for carbon-hungry on-demand fuel production. Additionally, these putative future control systems could combine into a system of systems that operates everything in concert. There are obvious dangers, but the potential of the Internet of Things is still being revealed.

Homes do not change much. We eat, sleep, and relax in much the same way as our ancestors have done for centuries. However, the home is nevertheless undergoing one of the biggest changes since the advent of plumbing, as we install more smart devices, all linked together on a home area network, or HAN.

97 NFTs

STANDING FOR NON-FUNGIBLE TOKENS, THIS TECHNOLOGY, closely allied with cryptocurrency, has gotten a bad name recently. However, NFTs and similar blockchain contracts might have applications beyond getting rich quick.

NFTs are sold as online works of art. However, the owner of the NFT has no rights over the distribution or viewing of the art. They own a unique piece of code associated with it. That is all.

A non-fungible token is a piece of code recorded on a blockchain in the same way as a coin of cryptocurrency. The difference is that it is unique and cannot be replaced. That is what "non-fungible" means. A crypto coin is not unique. One is exactly like the other. NFTs made headlines a few years ago as a way of buying ownership of a property that exists only as computer code. In 2021, the first tweet on Twitter was sold as an NFT for $2.9 million. The link to blockchains and crypto created an investment bubble in NFTs, which has long since burst. NFTs for this kind of thing are now worthless. However, NFTs and similar smart systems could simplify real-world contracts. A contract agreement is recorded on the blockchain and runs automatically. As soon as the product or service is completed according to agreement, payment is made. The supplier cannot be cheated out of their money, and the client only needs to pay if the supplier does the job right.

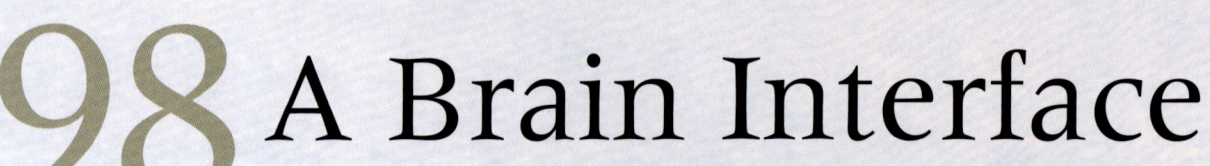

98 A Brain Interface

IT HAS BEEN KNOWN FOR 150 YEARS THAT THE BRAIN IS AN ELECTRICAL DEVICE. Attempts to make sense of its electrical output have been limited, but machine learning might soon create a computer–brain interface.

Have you ever had a brain wave? The answer is always yes, all the time. In the 1870s, it was discovered that brains produce a weakly fluctuating electrical field. In 1924, the electroencephalograph (EEG) machine was perfected to amplify these signals, creating a visual representation of electrical oscillations—or brain waves. The EEG's inventor saw the waves as a "brain mirror" that somehow represented psychic abilities, and true enough, the brain waves do change in character to match brain activity and states of awareness. As such, the EEG became a valued diagnostic tool indicating brain activity, but there was no direct link between the electrical signals and a particular brain function. The waves showed the full orchestra playing, and there was no way to isolate a single string on a violin.

In 2022, a U.S. company called Neuralink made headlines for implanting an electrical probe into the brains of animals. This has been an active research field for decades, but the headlines were due to the company's link to the controversial tech billionaire Elon

Fitting the probe is not without risk, so it is only performed on people who stand to benefit from it, such as those with physical impairments. As well as helping with mobility, the probe has potential for telepathic communication—transmitting thoughts.

Musk, as well as the fact that this illustrated how much progress machine learning techniques were making in decoding brain activity. A probe more sensitive than those used in EEGs is implanted in the brain, with electrodes passing through the skull. The patient then trains an AI by repeatedly thinking about something, such as a physical movement or a phrase. In most cases, the test subjects are people with profound physical disabilities, such as paralysis below the neck. The unsupervised machine learning is able to isolate the electrical signals that are the physical manifestation of mental activity. In one study carried out at Stanford University, the system was able to convert the subject's thoughts into written text. Neuralink has had monkeys playing ping-pong video games with thought alone, and its human program has big hopes for linking thoughts to the control of exoskeletons or other robotic aids. There are also plans to develop implants that work with visual signals. If the brain uses one code for all its activity (which is assumed), then implants could one day become a general computer interface.

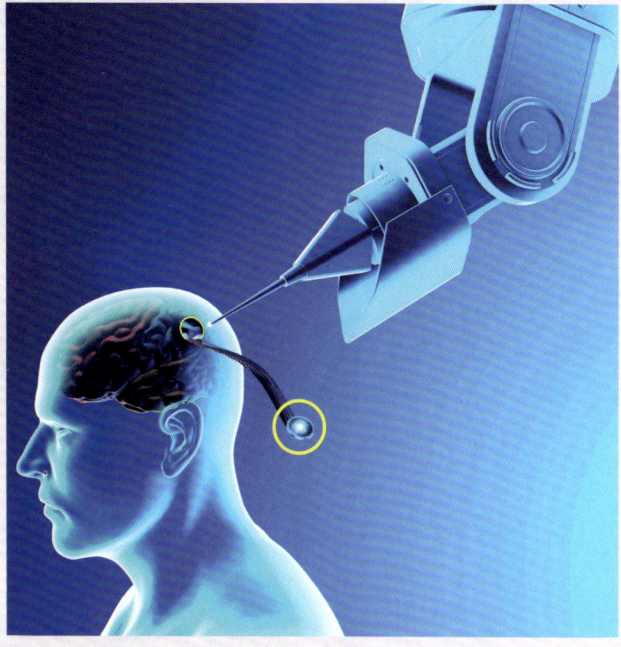

99 AlphaFold

AI IS GOING TO CHANGE THE WORLD. GOOGLE DEEPMIND made a big leap forward in 2022 with its protein-predicting AI.

Protein is perhaps not as exciting as a robot or brain-computer interface, but it is vital to life on Earth. All living things use proteins to build and run the body. There are 300 million in use across the biosphere, each with a unique shape that lets it do a highly specific job. The shape is coded in genes, which set out the exact order of building blocks, called amino acids, for each protein. This has been well-known for decades. However, no one has been able to calculate the shape of a protein from its amino acids. The final chain folds and wrinkles, and one change of amino acid could makes the whole shape reorganize in an unpredictable way. But now AlphaFold, a DeepMind AI, has used machine learning to crack it. There are 20 amino acids in nature, and the average protein has 300 acids, so there are about 10^{390} possible proteins. To date, AlphaFold has decoded 200,000 or so. A human researcher constructing each protein in the lab would need a billion years to reach this number! Cracking the protein code will help unlock the human genome and create new drugs to tackle disease.

Proteins are complex chemicals built from chains of smaller molecules called amino acids. One fault in a protein can lead to life-changing diseases.

100 Generative AI

WE ARE AT THE START OF THE NEXT CHANGE IN COMPUTING, and this could be the big one—the AI Revolution. The latest AI does not just spot patterns; it creates new ideas, text, video, and pictures. How smart is that?

"An AI programmer diligently coding, bringing the power of GPT to life." This is the caption written for this picture by a chatbot based on ChatGPT-4. One day, a future GPT might read this book and come up with something better to say.

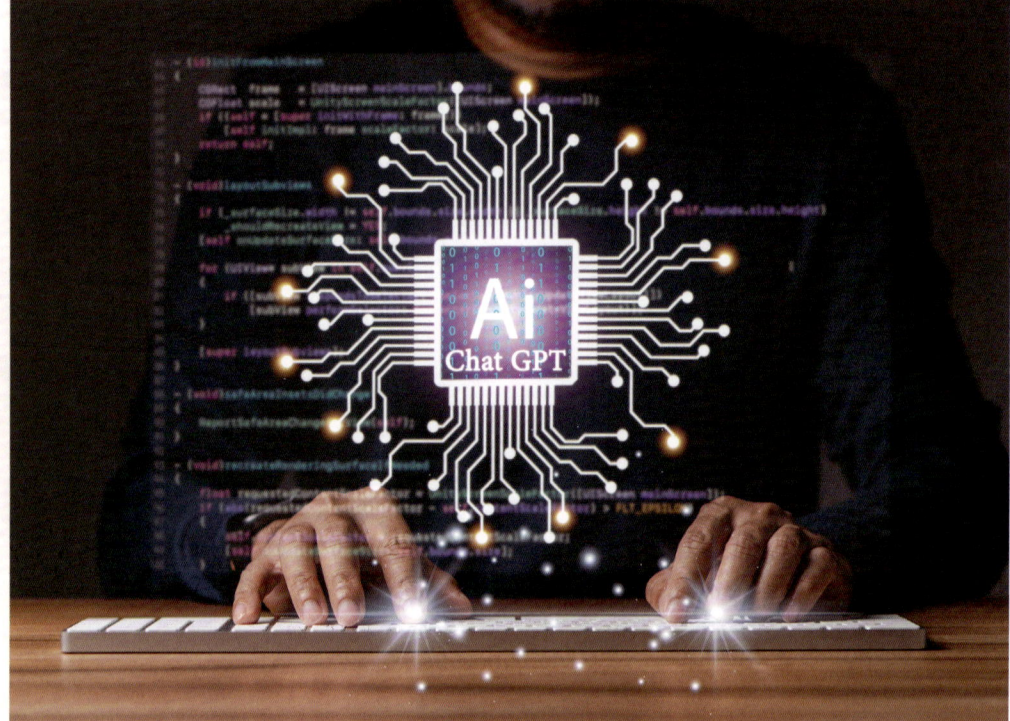

A kind of artificial intelligence called generative AI has been making rapid advances of late. For the general public, it represents a big leap forward in the capabilities of AI, and one that appeared to have happened very fast. For the AI industry, it has taken years, vast computing resources, and fierce competition to be a leader in the field. The abilities of generative AI are exciting and alarming to laypeople, but to experts and entrepreneurs, they represent an opportunity to transform the tech industry (and the world). A prize worth taking risks for, perhaps.

Large language models

Generative AIs have been trained to operate with complex systems, not least language. The first generative AI to go public was ChatGPT-4, made by OpenAI with support from Microsoft. GPT stands for Generative Pre-trained Transformer, and it is a language model that was trained on a reported 45 terabytes of text written by human

BIAS

No matter how smart an AI, there is always a risk that it is biased in some way. If that one AI is used to make decisions that affect people, that bias is magnified far more than those of a human decision maker. The bias can arise from incorrect or incomplete training data. There are several ways that can occur, but it is not always easy to see the bias beforehand. Only later, when the damage is done, is it apparent. One tool for spotting bias in AI is to test with counterfactual examples. This imagines that a person subject to the AI's processes belongs to a different group. If the AI is unbiased, then it gives the same response in both cases.

authors. Deep learning over months (and years if we count the earlier versions) created an algorithm that was adept at predicting the next word in a sentence. This ability is the main feature of generating accurate and fluent language—and reading it, too. While early forms of AI would label data according to its features, generative AI is able to generate features from labels. So a text prompt from a human is generated into a piece of writing. The language is flawless, although the facts may not be. It seems that generative AIs will "hallucinate." The AI is not lying, but makes stuff up to fill in gaps left after training.

Language models work with computer coding just as well, and generative AIs are able to write programs nearly as well as human coders. Language also allows the AI to understand what is in videos and pictures. AI image and video generators have been trained to link text with visual information, and can generate images from text prompts.

The dangers of AI

At the moment, generative AI is promoted as a way of searching the Web, writing reports, and creating other content. The most immediate danger is from fake content that we cannot tell from the real thing. What will society be like if we base our opinions on fake evidence (see page 124)? Perhaps more significant is the longer-term goal for generative AI. The technology will be developed not to generate content, but to generate possible futures. In other words, it will be an "artificial imagination" that predicts what is likely to happen next and make a plan of action accordingly. This is the kind of AI technology that will match the advances in robotics of recent years, creating robots and other machines that can operate without human supervision. What will we ask these robots and other AIs to do?

PERSONAL ASSISTANT

Generative AI is being developed as a powerful productivity tool. It can read emails, summarize meetings, and generate reports. One wonders what will be left for us to do. An AI assistant will be of benefit to executives and fee-earning professionals, but might prove a threat to support staff. Optimists point to previous technological revolutions, where automation creates more jobs for humans, not fewer. Others say that there is something different this time: AI automates intellectual work not physical labor.

Large language models and other GPTs are created through deep learning with large, unstructured data sets. The algorithm learns to calculate the chances of one feature of data being related to another.

101 Computer Science: the basics

COMPUTER HARDWARE HAS AN APPEAL ALL OF ITS OWN. The glow of a data center with its bundles of colored cables gives a sense of great power, and the gleam and heft of a new personal device is certainly a thrill. But we must not lose sight of what lies beneath: The software. From the basic tasks and everyday applications, like streaming and spreadsheets, all the way to AI, the real work is being done by the programming! Let's take a closer look at that.

The Life Cycle of a Program

Engineering code Programs are produced by coding professionals called software engineers. Like an engineer building a tunnel or designing a motor, software engineers work through a series of steps to develop programs—and their work is never-ending! Software development follows a cycle where new versions are launched to replace previous ones, adding improvements each time. This cyclical process ensures that the best program is produced in the shortest amount of time. It applies to any type of program—from firmware to apps—and can be carried out by a single coder or a worldwide team.

The process starts with a discovery phase where a set of functions and aims are set out by the team, who then also consider any problems they might face. Once a clearer plan for the project is in place, it enters the analysis phase. This is when the team figures out what they will need to do to progress and researches how their ideas could better focus on the end users of the software. Now it is time to design the program, a task led by a software architect. It is their role to break down the software functions into distinct modules and layers and show how they will link together in the finished product.

Now for the part you've all been waiting for. The stage when the software is written is called implementation. It is the job of software engineers, called developers. Each developer or team of developers will focus on a module of the overall design. They can use a range of programming languages (see page 123). Each module will need to be tested and debugged (see page 122), and eventually the whole software project will be ready to launch. Once in use, the software engineers are still needed to solve problems as they arise. They release quick fixes, called patches, and eventually return to the start to plan a better version. Off we go again!

LIFE CYCLE OF A PROGRAM

1. PLANNING
The team gathers for a "brainstorm," where people with different skills are invited to throw out ideas about who the software could be for and what it will do. The list generated is reduced to a set of core ideas within a plan of action. The team then considers whether implementing this plan has any obvious problems.

2. ANALYSIS
A business analyst will research the end users of the planned product to find out if it meets their needs or could be improved in that regard. This creates a model of an average user to aim the product at. Other analysts evaluate whether the system requirements of the planned product meet the needs of the customers.

3. DESIGN
The analysis is considered by the software architect, who then creates a high-level design. The program's functions are divided into modules. An architect might visualize the information, using charts to show data flow through the software, and decision trees to explain relationships between modules in the software. Sometimes the design is simulated to show how well it performs.

4. IMPLEMENTATION
In this coding phase, developers translate the high-level system design into actual source code. The best developers write code that is easy to understand. This generally means the code is also more efficient and easy to maintain. Developers use version control systems to keep track of all their changes and can reverse them if necessary.

5. TESTING & INTEGRATION
Before it is released to the public, the software is thoroughly tested. Generally, the developers will use testing software to generate reports on how each module is functioning. Errors are assessed and fixed accordingly, and then modules are integrated until the whole system is ready to be tested.

6. MAINTENANCE
The software is now released for use, but there will still be problems reported when the program is run on different systems. Developers will rewrite the code for certain modules that represent problems for security or stability, and make updates available for users. Software engineers also monitor how users perceive the software's performance.

Pseudocode Flowcharts

Visual tool Pseudocode is so-named because it works like a program, but does not use a formal programming language. This chart is a visual tool used to represent an algorithm using natural language. A developer will convert it into source code, assuming the pseudocode is good. That is kind of the point. The chart is a way of analyzing what the software is supposed to do—or another complicated process. The flowchart uses different shapes and arrows to depict the flow of data through operations. The arrows loop and divide as the process runs. Eventually, the control arrives at the end point—or if it does not, the pseudocode reveals that bug and can be modified. Pseudocode flow charts are a good way to understand complex processes. They require it to be broken down into simple steps. Any inefficiencies or bad assumptions will become clear. The flowchart's universal visual language makes it a good way for software engineers to work collectively on complex projects. Can you see any bugs in the chart opposite?

 **Start /End**

 **Input / Output**
Data enters or leaves the system here.

 **Process**
Something is done to the data at this stage.

 **Flow direction**
This is the direction taken by data, information, or control.

 Decision
A true-false or if-else statement leads to the flow dividing into two possible paths.

CONSTANTS AND VARIABLES

Coding works with data types called constants and variables. In some ways, they can be seen as boxes. A constant is a box that has been sealed shut. The value or data that it contains cannot be altered while the program runs. A variable is also a box, but this one it has its lid open, and data can be stored inside and moved from box to box as the program runs. The boxes also carry a label for the data. So a constant box could contain the number π, while a variable box holds the value for a radius. The program uses the variable and constant to calculate variables for other boxes, such as area and circumference.

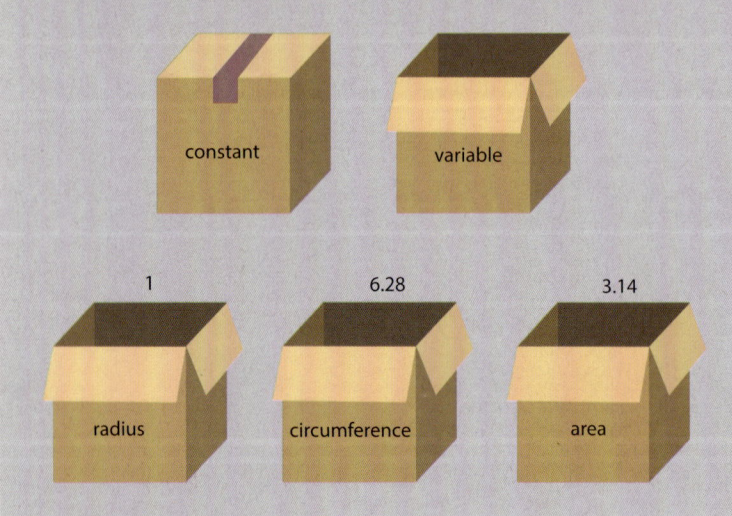

COMPUTER SCIENCE: THE BASICS * 121

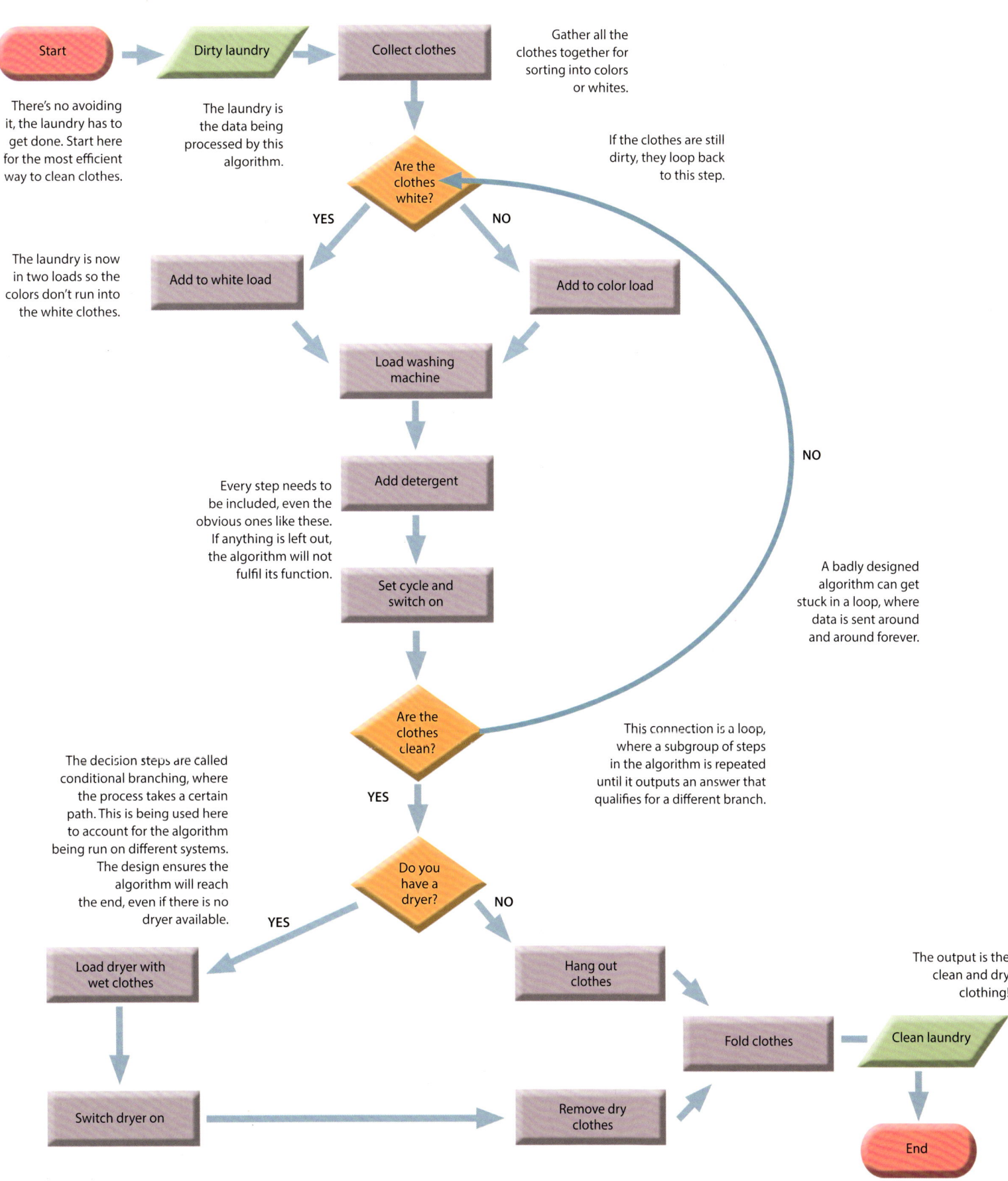

Testing and debugging

Solving problems Software is both tested and debugged to find problems with the program and fix them. However, they are both very different processes with different methods and aims. Software testing happens before debugging. It can be automated or done by hand and has several different aims, such as verifying that the software meets the technical requirements of its design. In "black box" testing, the software is checked only by comparing inputs with outputs. The source code is not available. In "white box" systems, the testers are looking at the internal code to see how it is acting. Debugging, on the other hand, is the process of fixing a bug in the software. It usually begins after the software has failed to execute in the expected way. Debugging involves analyzing the symptoms of a problem and identifying the root cause in the code. It is often done manually with a careful review of the code, but attempts are being made to automate it—perhaps with the help of AI.

SOFTWARE TESTING TYPES

USABILITY — These are tests for user-friendliness that ensure the design of the user interface is understood and navigable by all users. It gathers data on the user experience, which is fed back into the maintenance phase of the software cycle.

SECURITY — This kind of testing looks for vulnerabilities in the software application that could be exploited by hackers. It is a specialist task normally carried out by testers who were not involved in the original development. Often, the best testers are "white hats," or hackers, working to reduce malicious activity. (That is the sort of thing that "black hats" do!)

FUNCTIONAL — Functional testing looks at each unit or module of the software and then verifies how they work as they are integrated into the full system. The final system tests emulate real-world uses in a controlled environment. After this has been successfully completed, the final stage is acceptance testing.

PERFORMANCE — This area of testing monitors how a product allocates its resources, and how quickly it responds to inputs and generates outputs. It is linked to stability testing, in that the software may be less reliable when run on certain processors or operating systems. A performance test simulates real-world conditions that might reach the limits of the software.

STABILITY — Also called compatibility testing, this process involves checking that the product works just as well—or well enough—when run in different environments. The "environment" could refer to specific devices and operating systems, or it could mean the product is being viewed through a specific browser or another web app or platform, such as a smart TV. Software may pass its functional tests but be unstable in certain environments. This is a consideration for the software cycle. Do you debug? Or withdraw support for this problematic environment?

ACCEPTANCE — This is the final test of whether the software functions according to the technical requirements of its design. Tests validate that the software works with the minimum system requirements and meets the expectations of end users. This testing takes place in a real-world environment to ensure the simulations used until this point are not hiding problems.

Progamming languages

Three levels Programming languages conform to different levels. A low-level language is directly interacting with the hardware. Machine language is binary code, while assembly language is written for a specific design of microchip. High-level languages are more human-friendly because they use word-like commands in sentence-like code. Procedural language is for setting out a unique sequence of instructions. The earliest high-level codes were of this type. A functional language works with mathematical-type functions, which create more general steps than in a procedural language. This code is used for setting up machine learning. Logic languages build algorithms in symbolic logic using Boolean operations. These languages have uses in creating AI. A programmer uses object-oriented languages to build code from a toolkit of prepared "objects" for certain functions and data structures. Scripting languages are for automating repetitive tasks. This kind of code often runs inside other software, like a browser. Specialized languages have a niche purpose. A mark-up language is used to format information. A query language is used for managing databases. Other languages are purpose-built for a specific application.

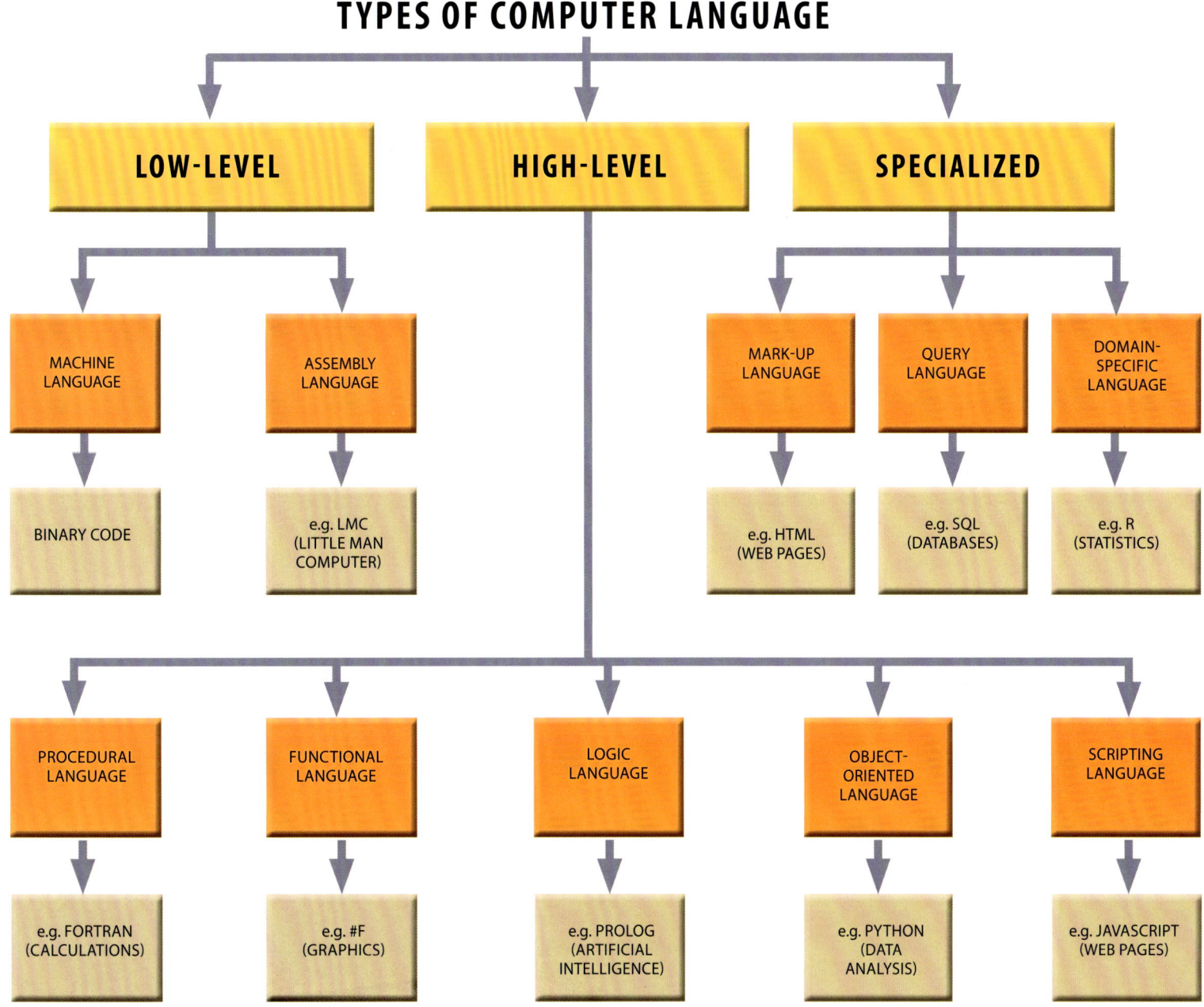

IMPONDERABLES

COMPUTERS ARE NOT NEW. EVERYONE READING THIS HAS LIVED IN AN AGE where computers have been a tool at work, at school—and now everywhere. In all that time, technology has been enacting change. What are the big questions about what happens next?

What is the Singularity?

The Technological Singularity is a future event where an AI reaches a level of intelligence that allows it to break free of human control. The AI rapidly consumes the abilities of other AIs in an "intelligence explosion," resulting in a superintelligence that far outstrips our own. What happens next? Answers depend on your outlook. If the AI really is so clever, maybe it will recognize the rights of all beings to live a natural life. That might be good; the AI looks after us. Another possibility is that it wipes us out—or harnesses us for labor. Either way, perhaps we should try to avoid it happening.

If the Technological Singularity occurred, how would we know? Could we detect it, or would it make itself known to us?

The problem of fake news

Seeing is believing, they say. As a civilization, we put great value in the things we see and hear—and, to a lesser extent, what other people tell us. Through its long history, news media has been a means for us to see and hear events that we were not personally witness to. The video, audio, and photography tell the story alongside the reporting of events. With the emergence of "deepfake" technology, AI threatens to create entirely fictitious events. It is still possible to spot fact from fake if you pay close enough attention, but the gap will only narrow.

Add to this explicit attempts to undermine the veracity of all news by political forces. This can be done by disseminating fake or obfuscated news. The fact that some news is obviously faked makes us distrust all news sources. Bad actors can dismiss actual evidence of their deeds as "fake news." To reinforce the problem, AI-driven personalization serves every user with news content that confirms their world view—and implicit biases. Within years, it will be possible to construct entirely false histories from faked evidence. Who can say which one is real? There are calls to watermark AI-generated content to prevent these issues, but in the end, the conspiracy theorists will have gotten one thing right (and only one thing): Do your own research!

Will future computing be green enough?

Climate models—run on a carbon-guzzling supercomputer—predict damaging climate changes if we don't fix our emissions.

The Internet is big—in every sense. It covers the world and links billions of devices. However, somehow, we forget all of that. Streaming movies from the comfort of our homes or messaging on the go, we seldom think beyond our own devices and services. So it might come as a surprise to find out that about 4 percent of carbon emissions (driving climate change, remember) come from the Internet. That is more than all the emissions from passenger flights. That is consumed in making the devices, of course, and the electricity we use to power them. However, the simple act of using a search engine leads to carbon emissions. Your search request travels through the Internet to a data center, where the search is actually carried out. These data centers have tens of thousands of computers, all drawing power but also giving out heat. Almost half of the power used in a data center is used to keep the computers cool. Along the way, the core routers and backbone cabling have a power demand, and the search engine is only really any good at the job because there are billions of other requests pinging around the rest of the Net, which the search algorithm is using to weigh up the results. Simply storing your data in the cloud emits greenhouse gases! By 2040, the Net's emissions are predicted to reach 14 percent as other industries become carbon neutral.

So what can be done? At home, the obvious thing to do is switch to a source of renewable electricity. You can also dim your monitor, shut down devices when not in use—even cutting back on replying to all emails has an effect! An email with seven recipients will release an ounce of carbon dioxide! And that figure goes up when you send big attachments. The biggest footprint from home users is streaming video. The tech companies have their part to play, and several aim to be carbon neutral by 2030. They can achieve this by building data centers with renewable power supplies—and in colder locations! Some data centers even harness their own heat to generate electricity.

Will we upload our minds?

If—and it's still only an if—our consciousness is formed by the physical activity of our brain's material, then your mind, in this instant, is just a of set information. And that data set could be captured, encoded, and replayed inside a computer. Would this device now be you? Or a version of you? Quantum physics makes it tricky for the computer to maintain a "you" that is a consciousness in the present, but let's say some clever software solves all that stuff. Would you take this option and live in a computer? It's a no-brainer, surely?

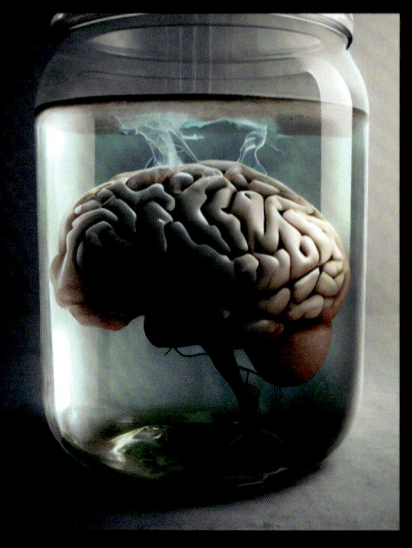

What kind of jar have you got in mind?

What is right and wrong in a virtual world?

Doing the wrong thing in the real world has consequences. Violence, damage, and theft have demonstrable effects on others, and so they are punished by the justice system. There is a vision of a virtual alternative reality, or metaverse, where people can visit, work, and play as entities called avatars. The laws of physics in the metaverse need not match those of the Universe. (We could fly or travel from place to place in an instant, for example.) But what about the laws of the land? Can an avatar be violent or threatening? Avatars feel no pain, so is harm in a virtual world actual harm? Who owns the virtual property in the metaverse? How could it be stolen permanently? Surely it could just be reset easily enough. All these questions suggest that life in a future metaverse lacks authenticity. It might be fun for a bit, but essentially, it would be an empty experience. If pain and suffering became a VR feature, would you enter that virtual world?

Virtual reality takes you to places beyond your reach or imagination.

Will electronics ever be superseded?

Electronics are facing a crisis. Transistors built from doped silicon crystals cannot get much smaller, and that means that for computing to become more powerful, the chips and devices need to get bigger. One trend is to keep the chips in your phone as they are (optimization will slow) and rely on the cloud to fulfill your services. That means building more data centers (with more carbon emissions, probably). Or we could develop new technologies for logic circuitry. Two possibilities are photonics and spintronics. The former uses laser beams instead of electric currents to represent a binary state. A photonic transistor is a crystal that can amplify or block a beam. Spintronics stores bits as the "spin" state of electrons. Transistors that use this phenomenon are faster and less energy-intensive. However, there is a long way to go before they will rival electronic ones.

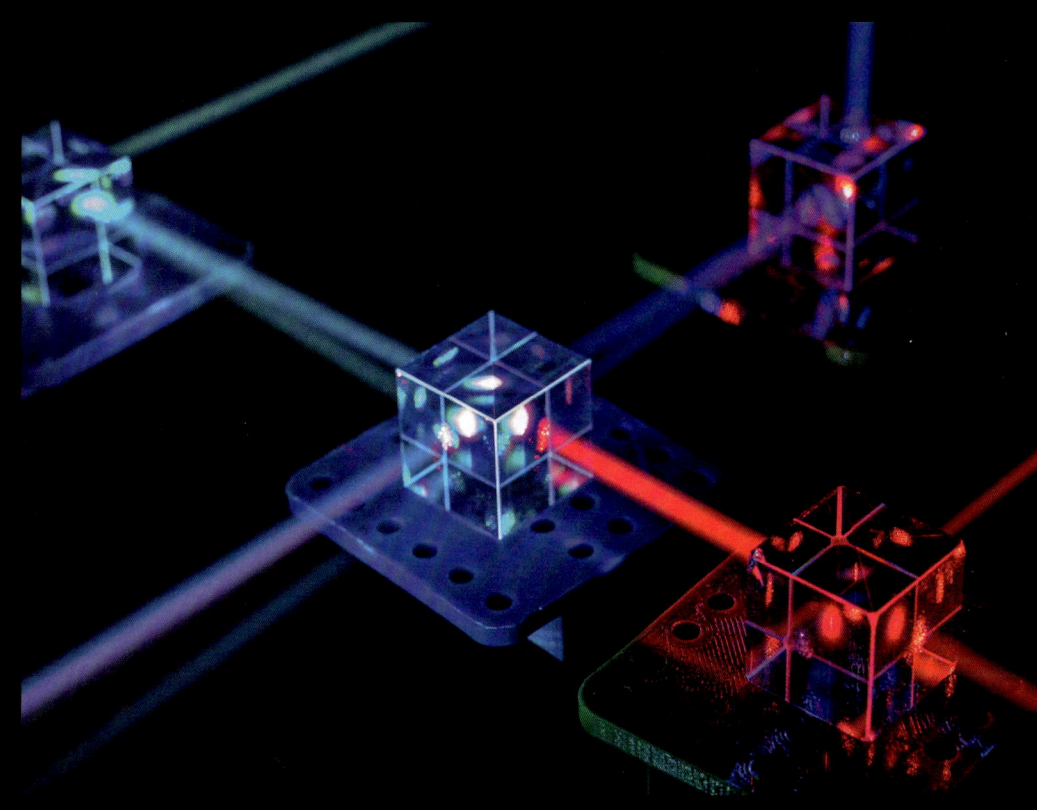

A computer of the future might process information as laser light, not electric current.

Will the Web be divided up?

The Internet is currently neutral and open to all.

The Internet was created neutral. That means that all the traffic passing through it is granted the same equal access. The backbones and routers do not favor some packets over others. The Internet Service Providers (ISPs) whom we pay for our connections are not supposed to discriminate against a type of user or type of content. For example, every customer pays the same connection fee irrespective of whether they stream movies or sports or look only at Facebook or YouTube. The ISP cannot (or should not) charge more for sports traffic than a movie stream. The reasoning behind this is to ensure that ISPs do not filter the content to suit the highest payers. That would create a closed network that blocks out those who cannot afford to be seen and heard. Neutrality fosters free speech and also gives disruptive start-ups a chance to take on established providers. ISPs do, of course, filter illegal content, such as abuse and threats, and there is an ongoing debate about what constitutes illegal content that must be removed.

IMPONDERABLES

Is a strong AI our equal?

A strong AI is another term for AGI, or artificial general intelligence. The term strong AI arises from the Chinese Room Argument (see page 71). In a nutshell, it indicates that an AI has some awareness and is able to understand the limits of its own intelligence. The threshold for AGI is set at being the equal of human intelligence, but strong AI could be given a wider meaning. A strong AI need not be as clever as us, but might be the equal of a dog, chimpanzee, or crow (they are surprisingly smart)—as long as it is aware of its limits. A strong AI could push back those limits by learning new skills, but let's assume there is an upper ceiling on the processing power available to it—its brain is of finite size, like ours. So this is a being that has some awareness and intelligence. It might not be our equal in intelligence, but do we have dominion over it? We would be its owners perhaps, like we own animals and have the ultimate say over their welfare. Now imagine if that strong AI was at least as clever as us—perhaps smarter—but still functioned according to our commands. Do we still own that AI? Or does it become a person, if not literally, then in law?

Whose home is this?

What will happen to privacy?

Whether we like it or not, we pay for free services on the Web with our private information. When we click "Agree," we permit ISPs, apps, and web platforms to collect data about our activities, including the ones we would keep hidden from our friends and family. What if we chose not to agree? It is getting harder—nigh-on impossible—for us to give consent every time our data is captured. So what happens next? In the worst case scenario, users have no control over their data, but have no off-line option to access vital services. The data becomes a tool of political control, and democratic processes are undermined. Another scenario is that it is possible to opt out of data mining for a fee. This effectively makes privacy something that has to be purchased, not an essential right. The third scenario sees governments stepping in to control how data is collected and used, with varying regimes used across the world. This stifles innovation. The fourth possible future is one where people have direct control over their data, wherever it is stored. They therefore trust companies to use it well and agree to it being used in return for services.

Our location and search history is collected across all our devices, although our messages mostly remain private.

How will technology change education?

Artificial intelligence is already being used in the classroom, with perhaps good and bad results. First, the bad news. Chatbots can write reports and fool teachers into thinking students have a grasp of a topic when they have not engaged at all. However, teachers can also use the AI to create engaging educational content. Imagine a video recreation of a historical event or a VR view of a chemical reaction. The world's leading experts can give lessons to millions via video conference. And AI can also be used to spot fake assignments from real ones!

Technology can be used for learning as well as for fun!

How will the Internet change?

Beyond the Wi-Fi router, the Internet is all cable—millions of miles of it (or more!). Outside, we get our connectivity through the cellular network. The latest 5G service offers download speeds that can supersede a home connection, but it requires more cell towers closer together (although they are admittedly smaller, too). We can't cover the whole planet in cell towers and cables, so to really build fast Internet worldwide, we will need to look up. Satellite Internet services, such as Starlink, are already offering fast connections almost anywhere on Earth—including remote places where cables will not reach. The space-based services use constellations of thousands of small(ish) satellites, each weighing about a quarter of a ton, orbiting a few hundred miles above the planet. But by solving one problem, the satellites create another. There are so many of them that they are interfering with astronomical observations.

How would your life change if you always had an Internet connection?

IMPONDERABLES

What will AI do to freedom of speech?

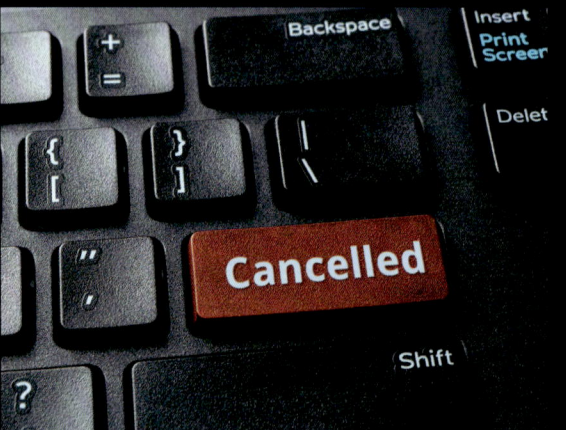

The analytical powers of generative AI create a double-edged sword for people getting their news and entertainment online. Already, AIs are busy looking for dangerous, abusive, and inappropriate material posted on social media. That technology maintains our freedom from being exposed to explicit material that would cause us harm. However, if we rely too heavily on AI to moderate content on our behalf, we risk forms of speech being suppressed without us even knowing it. This already happens to a certain extent within the "content bubbles" that are created by the personalization of our social media fields. The kinds of content, including opinions, that we have actively rejected in the past will not be served up as often, if at all. So strangely, AI will not suppress freedom of speech so much as freedom to hear.

It is all too easy to simply block a person and never hear from them again—ever. But that's a big move, one not to be taken lightly.

Can we escape the Uncanny Valley?

As we endeavor to make robots that look and behave more like living things, something strange happens. As the device is made to look more alive, it takes on an eerie look and begins to disgust us. This downturn in our attitude is called the Uncanny Valley. It is probably a response to our acute sense of danger. The uncanny device sets off our deep-seated alarm. It looks recognizable as a living thing, but lacks a certain vital spirit. All this adds up to us feeling disturbed, wanting to get away from a potential source of danger, and feeling sick, even, as the body prepares to purge itself of toxins. So that's a bit of a problem. What can we do to get out of the Uncanny Valley? There are two sources of the disturbance—movement and looks. Robots that move in a smooth and controlled way are more appealing. When it comes to looks, robot faces can pull many expressions, but it might be better to simply avoid trying to emulate the skin and hair. Let the robot be a robot!

Which one of these robots makes you most uneasy?

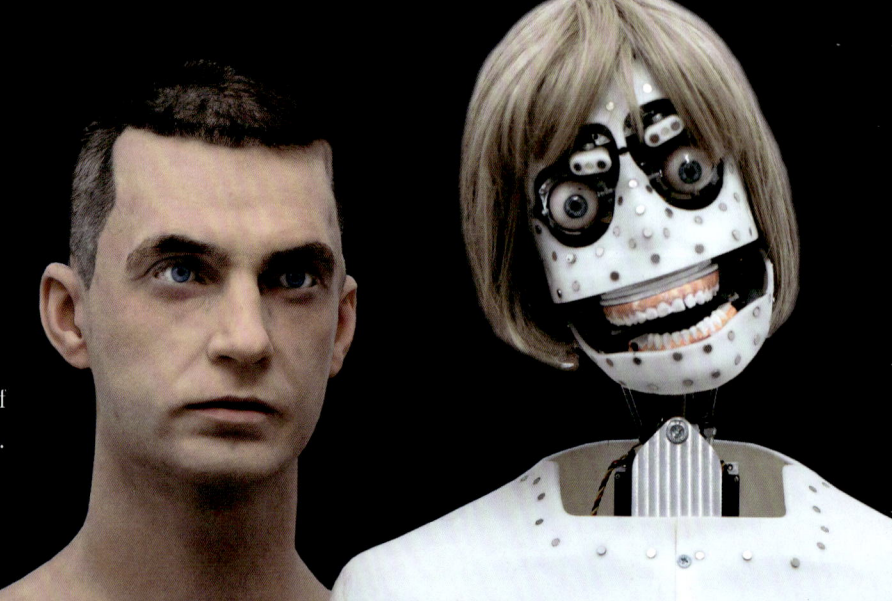

If this hacker is so clever, why can't they turn the heating on?

Will hackers be defeated?

Some of the most common hacks rely as much on human nature as they do on computer know-how. Hackers use confidence tricks to get into your device. They might call up in the guise of a technical support worker from a bank or ISP and simply ask for your password and login details. It works sometimes! There are nearly a million cyber attacks each year, and around 95 percent are from human error. The target lets the hacker in, perhaps by clicking on a Trojan to unleash a virus. Machine learning is used to train AIs to check for spam and malware in emails and web pages. It's getting better all the time—especially if you help train it by correcting its mistakes. An increasing use of biometrics for authenticating identity also helps. Similarly, two-factor security, where a login is confirmed with a second device, is a powerful barrier as well.

More well-organized hackers will target bigger victims, such as companies and public agencies. They can use ransomware to hold the organization's data hostage. Ordinary people may be impacted by this kind of attack, both in the real world and through the withdrawal of online services. In many cases, the attacks are relatively simple. A USB drive is inserted into a networked computer, and malware gets in that way. Large organizations may have older computers, which are easier to exploit. It's important to keep your software up-to-date. A lot of the time, those updates are patching up weaknesses discovered in the software.

Looking to the future, it is probable that quantum computing will make password-based security too weak to use. Instead, we will rely on biometrics. However, public-key encryption methods would still be effectively uncrackable. Another form of quantum computing—quantum cryptography—might also make it completely impossible for anyone to access any communication without it being spotted. The system encodes the message—a public key, for example—as a quantum state, and that state collapses when it is read. If the state of the message is not as expected when received, then we know a snooper has been at work.

The Great Computer Scientists

Every successful technology changes things, but computing is one of the significant ones. Compared to the pantheon of great inventions (like writing, motive power, etc.), computers have been the most powerful agents of change. And this is illustrated by the life stories of the people that made it all possible (among the contributions of thousands of others). Many of them were working within living memory, and several are still young people who no doubt have much more to do.

George Boole

Born	November 2, 1815
Birthplace	Lincoln, England
Died	December 8, 1864
Importance	Invented Boolean algebra and logic

This English logician's genius was apparent early in life. He grew up in a meager home, and was given extracurricular schooling by his father and friends of the family. However, he largely taught himself, learning several languages from books and even mastering calculus (eventually). By the tender age of 16, the young George was a teacher himself, becoming the best-paid member of the family. Boole's success as a teacher did not go unnoticed, and in 1849 he was made the first math professor at a new university in Cork, Ireland, which is where he completed his work on symbolic logic.

Charles Babbage

Born	December 26, 1791
Birthplace	London, England
Died	October 18, 1871
Importance	Invented first mechanical computer

As a student, Babbage is reported to have been disappointed with the math teaching at Cambridge University and, inspired by the work of Leibniz and Lagrange, set up the Analytical Club with John Herschel (of the astronomical family) and others. As was quite normal for men of science in his day, Babbage was also a leading figure in the Ghost Club, which investigated the supernatural. He decided to design a mechanical computer because of all the errors made by human mathematicians. However, the sheer number of precision gears required made the device prohibitively expensive.

Ada Lovelace

Born	December 10, 1815
Birthplace	London, England
Died	November 27, 1852
Importance	Invented first computer program

Daughter of the notorious Romantic poet Lord Byron, Ada Lovelace was taught math from an early age, partly because her mother wanted Ada to avoid the madness believed to have afflicted Byron. Having married the Earl of Lovelace, Ada met Charles Babbage, inventor of the Analytical Engine. Invited by Babbage to translate an article about his machines, Lovelace added ideas of her own, including a way of programming the engine to compute Bernoulli numbers. Because of this, she is widely celebrated as the inventor of the first computer program.

John Ambrose Fleming

Born	November 29, 1849
Birthplace	Lancaster, England
Died	April 18, 1945
Importance	Invented first thermionic valve

Fleming was the eldest son of a clergyman and had an excellent education, eventually becoming a member of the faculty at Cambridge University in 1888. He was one of the first professors of electrical engineering and consulted for  Marconi and Edison, among other tech leaders of the day. Fleming patented the thermionic valve, or vacuum tube, in 1904. He also designed the radio transmitter with which the first transatlantic radio transmission was made, and established the right-hand rule used to visualize the field lines and currents in electromagnetism.

Vannevar Bush

Born	March 11, 1890
Birthplace	Everett, Massachusetts, USA
Died	June 28, 1974
Importance	Designer of analog computers

After earning a doctorate in electrical engineering in 1916, awarded jointly by MIT and Harvard University, Bush spent most of the next two decades at MIT developing new technology. During World War II, Bush headed the U.S. Office of Scientific Research and Development (OSRD), through which almost all  wartime military research was carried out. This included important developments in radar and the initiation and early administration of the Manhattan Project. He emphasized the importance of scientific research for national security and economic well-being.

Herman Hollerith

Born	February 29, 1860
Birthplace	Buffalo, New York, USA
Died	November 17, 1929
Importance	Founding figure of IBM

The son of German immigrants, Hollerith was a prodigy. He graduated from the Columbia School of Mines with an Engineer of Mines degree in 1879, at the age of 19. (His tabulating system of 1890 earned him a doctorate.) In 1882, Hollerith joined MIT to teach mechanical engineering. He patented a prototype of his punched card tabulating machine in 1884. The invention transformed data processing, and Hollerith founded a company to exploit his technology. This company was later amalgamated with several others and, in 1924, became International Business Machines, or IBM.

John von Neumann

Born	December 28, 1903
Birthplace	Budapest, Hungary
Died	February 8, 1957
Importance	Developer of computing architecture

It was obvious from an early age that Janos Neumann was a clever child. He could speak ancient Greek at the age of six and divide eight-digit numbers into each other. He proceeded to be the youngest, brightest, and best at every institution he passed through, from Budapest to Zurich and Berlin, before arriving at Princeton in the 1930s, renaming himself John and working alongside Albert Einstein. As well as developing computer architecture, von Neumann's work made valuable contributions to game theory.

Tommy Flowers

Born	December 22, 1905
Birthplace	London, England
Died	October 28, 1998
Importance	Creator of first electronic computer

The son of a bricklayer, Flowers began work as an apprentice in mechanical engineering at the Royal Arsenal in east London. He was also taking evening classes and soon earned a degree in electrical engineering. At the age of 21, Flowers joined the telecommunications division of the General Post Office, soon ending up as part of the research unit. He became a pioneer of an all-electric phone network. During World War II, Flowers designed and built Colossus, the world's first programmable electronic computer. This device is argued to have shortened the war by two years.

William Shockley

Born	February 13, 1910
Birthplace	London, England
Died	August 12, 1989
Importance	Co-inventor of the transistor

The son of mining engineers, William Shockley studied physics at Caltech and MIT, before joining Bell Laboratories to research electronics. He led the team that won the Nobel Prize for developing the transistor. Notoriously difficult to work with, Shockley moved to Mountain View, California, to be near his mother. There, he set up the first electronics plant in what became known as Silicon Valley. Many people who once worked for him led the area's involvement in electronics and computing. Shockley became an increasingly controversial figure.

Grace Hopper

Born	December 9, 1906
Birthplace	New York City, USA
Died	January 1, 1992
Importance	Developed early programming language

After a spell as a mathematics professor at Vassar College in New York, Hopper tried to join the U.S. Navy during World War II, but was only let into the Reserves. In 1944, she was involved in the development of the Harvard Mark 1 computer, and this led to further work on the UNIVAC, the first commercial computer. Hopper built an early compiler—software that created the machine code, or 1s and 0s, that the computer understood. This led Hopper to be a key figure in the 1950s development of COBOL, one of the first and most influential high-level programming languages.

Konrad Zuse

Born	June 22, 1910
Birthplace	Berlin, Germany
Died	December 18, 1995
Importance	Built first digital computer

After completing school, Zuse studied civil engineering and architecture at the Technical University of Berlin. He then became a design engineer at the Henschel aircraft factory. He found the manual calculations required for this job tedious and imagined a machine that could automate them. Zuse's greatest achievement was the world's first working programmable computer, the Z3, completed in May 1941. The electromechanical design proved slow and impractical. Nevertheless, the next model, Z4, received orders from the Nazi regime, but was not completed until 1950.

Alan Turing

Born	June 23, 1912
Birthplace	London, England
Died	June 7, 1954
Importance	Founding figure in digital computing

It is likely Alan Turing suffered from a form of autism, which made it hard for him to connect with others. After developing the model for digital computing, he then invented the Turing Test for artificial intelligence—if a computer could fool a human into thinking it is also human, it passes the test. (No one really thinks that now.) Turing was a member of the British government's science community. When he was arrested for a homosexual act—a crime in the early 1950s—his security clearance was revoked. Around two years later, Turing committed suicide by eating a poisoned apple.

Douglas Engelbart

Born	January 30, 1925
Birthplace	Portland, Oregon, USA
Died	July 2, 2013
Importance	Inventor of the GUI

Breaking his studies to serve as a radar technician during World War II, Engelbart completed a degree in electrical engineering in 1948, and had a PhD by 1955. Engelbart is best known for his contributions in the field of human-computer interaction. His work in the 1950s led to his patent for the computer mouse and the development of the basic graphical user interface (GUI). He also helped create groupware—applications that helped teams collaborate. These were all part of Engelbart's vision of how networked computers would one day connect us.

Claude Shannon

Born	April 30, 1916
Birthplace	Petoskey, Michigan, USA
Died	February 24, 2001
Importance	Developed logical circuits

Armed with a degree in mathematics and electrical engineering, and a PhD from MIT, Shannon began his career at Bell Labs in 1941, contributing to work on anti-aircraft missile systems. He stayed at Bell Labs until 1972, as well as working at MIT as a professor. Shannon's contributions were sealed well before this, while he was a student of Vannevar Bush at MIT. His master's thesis of 1940 is the founding document of information theory. This work used Boolean algebra to establish the underpinnings of digital circuits, which became fundamental to the operation of today's computers and telecommunications equipment.

Gladys West

Born	October 27, 1930
Birthplace	Sutherland, Virginia, USA
Died	–
Importance	Computer modeller

West grew up in a rural community, and worked hard at her school studies to secure a scholarship in mathematics at Virginia State. In 1956, West was one of four African Americans working at the U.S. Naval Proving Ground, first doing math by hand and then with computers. In 1978, West became project manager for a satellite studying the oceans. This project led to her working on Geosat, a satellite that could map Earth's surface. West and her team created a precise model of the planet's shape, which was used by the Global Positioning System (GPS) to make it as accurate as possible.

Frances E. Allen

Born	August 4, 1932
Birthplace	Peru, New York, USA
Died	August 4, 2020
Importance	Software pioneer

Having excelled at college in mathematics, Allen joined IBM Research as a programmer in 1957. Her first role was to train staff on Fortran, but she was later assigned to Harvest, a codebreaking project with the National Security Agency. Her work on Harvest focused on the compiler, and over the next decade or so, Allen became a world-leading figure in developing better compilers and methods of optimizing programming languages and software in general. She was the first woman to become an IBM Fellow in 1989, and in 2006 she became the first woman ever to win the prestigious Turing Award (computing's "Nobel Prize").

Margaret Hamilton

Born	August 17, 1936
Birthplace	Paoli, Indiana, USA
Died	–
Importance	Wrote Apollo spacecraft guidance software

One of Hamilton's first jobs was working on early computer modelling of weather and climate at MIT. She soon joined the Semi-Automatic Ground Environment (SAGE) project, the first U.S. air defense system. She wrote the software used to identify enemy aircraft from radar signatures. Hamilton then began contributing to NASA's moonshot. She led a team that developed the software for the guidance systems of the Apollo spacecraft. Hamilton is credited with coining the term "software engineer." She argued her team's work was just as important as those who built the spacecraft.

Annie Easley

Born	April 23, 1933
Birthplace	Birmingham, Alabama, USA
Died	June 25, 2011
Importance	Computer scientist at NASA

Easley grew up wanting to be a nurse, but shifted her vision to pharmacology in her teens. She never completed this degree (but later earned a degree in math in 1977 after studying part-time). After marrying and having children, Easley got a job as a "computer" at what soon became NASA. She later became a computer scientist, one of the first African-Americans to do that job at the space agency. She used computing to research rocket power and also studied the utility of renewable energy sources, EVs and hybrid vehicles.

Bob Kahn

Born	December 23, 1938
Birthplace	New York City, USA
Died	–
Importance	Co-developer of TCP/IP system

After completing a doctorate in electrical engineering, Kahn worked at Bell Labs for a while before becoming an assistant professor at MIT. He then became a consultant engineer working on the ARPANET. In 1972, Kahn came up with the initial ideas for what later became the Transmission Control Protocol (TCP), which was intended as a replacement for an earlier network protocol, NCP, used in the ARPANET. Along with Vinton Cerf, he is known for proposing TCP and the Internet Protocol (IP), the fundamental communication rules at the heart of the Internet. He won a Turing Award in 2004.

Vinton Cerf

Born	June 23, 1943
Birthplace	New Haven, Connecticut, USA
Died	–
Importance	Co-developer of TCP/IP system

While studying for a PhD at UCLA, Cerf worked under Leonard Kleinrock's data packet networking group that connected the first two nodes of the ARPANET, the precursor to the Internet. It was during this time that he met Bob Kahn, who was working on the ARPANET system architecture. Along with Kahn, Cerf is recognized as one of "the fathers of the Internet." Together, they co-designed the TCP/IP protocols, which are the fundamental communication protocols running the Net. He won a Turing Award in 2004. In 2005, Cerf was awarded the Presidential Medal of Freedom. Since then, he has been a vice president of Google.

Geoffrey Hinton

Born	December 6, 1947
Birthplace	London, England
Died	–
Importance	Pioneer of deep learning

This British-Canadian scientist is referred to as the "godfather of AI." In Britain, Hinton completed a degree in experimental psychology and a PhD in artificial intelligence, before moving to Toronto University. His contribution to AI took hold in the 1980s, when he was a leading advocate of

using backpropagation algorithms for training neural networks—now called deep learning. In 2013, Hinton started working for Google's AI division. In 2023, Hinton resigned from this role so he would be free to raise in public his concerns about the future risks of generative AI technology.

Whitfield Diffie

Born	June 5, 1944
Birthplace	Washington, D.C., USA
Died	–
Importance	Cryptographer

Known as Whit, Diffie developed an interest in cryptography at a young age. Ten years after graduating from MIT with a degree in mathematics, Diffie invented a method of public-key cryptography, along with Martin Hellman and Ralph Merkle. The collaborators introduced a method, known as the Diffie–Hellman key exchange, that solved the problem of encryption over the Internet. Diffie has spent many years working in security for Sun Microsystems, and as an Internet administrator and academic at Stanford University. He won a Turing Award in 2015.

Steve Wozniak

Born	August 11, 1950
Birthplace	San Jose, California, USA
Died	–
Importance	Co-founder of Apple Inc.

Wozniak showed a keen interest in electronics from an early age, designing electronic devices and games while still in his teens. In 1971, Wozniak designed the "Blue Box," a device for phreaking (or hacking telephone networks). With Steve Jobs, a friend from high school, he began to sell it to students in Berkeley, California. In 1976, the pair set up Apple Inc. Wozniak designed the Apple I and Apple II products, the latter becoming the first successful microcomputer. While still an Apple employee, Wozniak devotes most of his time to promoting careers in technology to schoolchildren.

Steve Jobs

Born	February 24, 1955
Birthplace	San Francisco, USA
Died	October 5, 2011
Importance	Co-founder of Apple Inc.

In his trademark black turtleneck sweater, Steve Jobs became the stereotype of a technology entrepreneur. With Syrian heritage, Jobs was adopted as a child and grew up in California. He dropped out of college to start Apple Inc. in 1976. The Apple computer was based on a design by his business partner, Steve Wozniak. Under Jobs's leadership, Apple became a major player in computing and communication technology, with products including the iPhone and the iPad. He also developed computer animation with the movie studio Pixar. Jobs died from cancer aged just 56.

Bill Gates

Born	October 28, 1955
Birthplace	Seattle, Washington, USA
Died	–
Importance	Co-founder of Microsoft

Bill Gates wrote his first computer program at the age of 13 on his school's new computer. After studying at Harvard, he dropped out in order to found a software company called Microsoft with his colleague Paul Allen. They wrote the BASIC program for the Altair 8800 before going on to supply the operating system for PCs and creating the software for the Windows operating system. Microsoft made Gates one of the world's wealthiest men, and he set up the world's largest charitable foundation to promote public health in the developing world. A recent success was his support for a malaria vaccine.

Tim Berners-Lee

Born	June 8, 1955
Birthplace	London, England
Died	–
Importance	Inventor of the World Wide Web

With parents who were both pioneers of computing science in the decades after World War II, it was almost inevitable that Tim Berners-Lee would follow in their footsteps. Working at CERN in Geneva, Switzerland, Berners-Lee created what he called the World Wide Web. In 1990, Berners-Lee built the world's first website, in which he described how the Web worked. It was later selected as the most important cultural moment in world history. Berners-Lee made the Web available for free to all users. Since then, Berners-Lee has taught at Oxford and MIT.

Larry Page

Born	March 26, 1973
Birthplace	East Lansing, Michigan, USA
Died	–
Importance	Co-founder of Google

Famous as one of the co-founders of Google along with Sergey Brin, Larry Page grew up in a home full of computers, as both his parents were among the early generation of computer scientists. Page began using computers at age six, in addition to proving to be a talented musician. After graduating from the University of Michigan, Page enrolled for a PhD at Stanford, where he involved Brin in his search for developing a method of ranking web pages. As CEO of Google, Page became notorious for his relentless desire to improve the search engine. He stepped down from this role in 2019.

Sergey Brin

Born	August 21, 1973
Birthplace	Moscow, Russia
Died	–
Importance	Co-founder of Google

Moving with his parents from the communist Soviet Union, Sergey Brin arrived in Maryland at the age of six. He followed his father in studying mathematics and computer science, first in Maryland and then at Stanford. At Stanford, Brin met Larry Page, with whom he created an algorithm to rank websites in order of their likely importance. Initially constructed in the pair's college dorm rooms, the service later became Google. Google made Brin one of the world's richest people and enabled him to pursue other interests, including energy and vehicle technologies that tackle climate change.

Mark Zuckerberg

Born	May 14, 1984
Birthplace	White Plains, New York, USA
Died	–
Importance	Co-founder of Facebook

At the age of just 12, Mark Zuckerberg built a computer messaging service to allow his dentist father to be informed by reception when his patients arrived. Zuckerberg remained fascinated by computers. He built games and music software and received education from a private tutor. At Harvard, he developed software to help students select their courses and also a social networking project called Harvard Connection. This prompted Zuckerberg to start what would become Facebook in 2004. Since then, Zuckerberg has dominated social media by purchasing Instagram and WhatsApp.

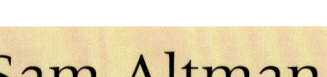

Demis Hassabis

Born	July 27, 1976
Birthplace	London, England
Died	–
Importance	Co-founder of Google DeepMind

Born in London of Greek Cypriot and Chinese Singaporean descent, Hassabis was a child prodigy in chess, reaching master standard at the age of just 13. At the age of 17, he began creating AIs for computer games, before getting a degree in computer science at Cambridge and a PhD in neuroscience from University College London. In 2010, Hassabis co-founded DeepMind (later acquired by Google). He was instrumental in the development of AlphaGo (which beat the world champion go player, a notoriously complicated game) and later AlphaFold. In 2024, Hassabis was knighted for services to AI.

Sam Altman

Born	April 22, 1985
Birthplace	Chicago, Illinois, USA
Died	–
Importance	Pioneer of generative AI

Altman received his first computer at the age of eight. As well as learning how to program, he also liked to take the computer apart to understand it better. He won a place at Stanford University to study computer science, but as is *de rigueur* among his kind, he soon dropped out. At the age of 27, Altman had already sold a mobile app for millions and was the president of Y Combinator, an investment platform for tech start-ups. In 2019, Altman became the CEO of OpenAI, the company that led the way in the generative AI revolution. All eyes are now on Altman as that revolution accelerates.

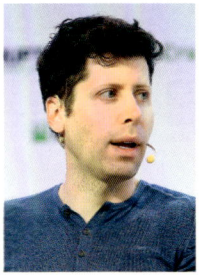

BIBLIOGRAPHY AND OTHER RESOURCES

Books

Abelson, Harold and Gerald Jay Sussman. *Structure and Interpretation of Computer Programs*. MIT Press, 2022.

Bernhardt, Chris. *Quantum Computing for Everyone*. MIT Press, 2019.

Bonaventure, Olivier. *Computer Networking: Principles, Protocols and Practice*. Lulu, 2016.

Brooks, Frederick P., Jr. *The Mythical Man-Month: Essays on Software Engineering*. Addison Wesley, 1995.

Cormen, Thomas H., Charles E. Leiserson, Ronald L. Rivest, and Clifford Stein. *Introduction to Algorithms*. MIT Press, 2022.

Hunt, Andrew and David Thomas. *The Pragmatic Programmer*. Pearson, 2019.

Levy, Steven. *Hackers: Heroes of the Computer Revolution*. O'Reilly, 2010.

Martin, Robert C. *Clean Code: A Handbook of Agile Software Craftsmanship*. Prentice Hall, 2008.

Mollick, Ethan. *Co-Intelligence: Living and Working with AI*. Portfolio/Penguin, 2024.

Petzold, Charles. *The Annotated Turing: A Guided Tour Through Alan Turing's Historic Paper on Computability and the Turing Machine*. Wiley, 2008.

Provost, Foster and Tom Fawcett. *Data Science for Business*. O'Reilly, 2013.

Russell, Stuart and Peter Norvig. *Artificial Intelligence: A Modern Approach*. Pearson, 2022.

Seibel, Peter. *Coders at Work: Reflections on the Craft of Programming*. Apress, 2009.

Sipser, Michael. *Introduction to the Theory of Computation*. Gengage, 2014.

Suleyman, Mustafa. *The Coming Wave: Technology, Power, and the Twenty-first Century's Greatest Dilemma*. Crown, 2023.

Vogelstein, Fred. *Battle of the Titans: How the Fight to the Death Between Apple and Google is Transforming our Lives (Dogfight)*. William Collins, 2013.

Apps

Code.org

Github

Mimo: Learn Coding/Programming

Programming Hub

Archives

Charles Babbage Institute Archives, University of Minnesota, Minneapolis, USA

Charles Babbage records, National Archives, Kew, London, UK

George Boole archive, Royal Society, London, UK

Vannevar Bush papers, Library of Congress, Washington, D.C., USA

John Ambrose Fleming Archive, University College London, UK

Margaret Hamilton papers, National Air and Space Museum, Smithsonian, Washington, D.C., USA

Herman Hollerith papers, Library of Congress, Washington, D.C., USA

Grace Murray Hopper Collection, National Museum of American History, Smithsonian, Washington, D.C., USA

Ada Lovelace papers, Bodleian Libraries, University of Oxford, UK

Claude Elwood Shannon Collected Papers, Massachusetts Institute of Technology Libraries, Cambridge, MA, USA

William Shockley Papers, Stanford University, California, USA library.stanford.edu

Alan Turing Collection, King's College, University of Cambridge, UK

Museums and Places to Visit

American Computer & Robotics Museum, Bozeman, Montana, USA

Apple Museum, Savona, Italy

Apple Park Visitor Center, San José, California, USA

Canada Science and Technology Museum, Ottawa, Canada

Centre for Computing History, Cambridge, UK

China Science and Technology Museum, Beijing, China

City of Science and Industry, Paris, France

Computer History Museum, Mountain View, California, USA

Computer History Museum Slovenia, Ljubljana, Slovenia

Computer Museum NAM-IP, Namur, Belgium

Computer Museum of America, Roswell, Georgia, USA

Deutsches Museum, Munich, Germany

Heinz Nixdorf MuseumsForum, Paderborn, Germany

HomeComputerMuseum, Helmond, The Netherlands

Intel Museum, Santa Clara, California, USA

KCG Computer Museum, Kyoto, Japan

Microsoft Visitor Center, Redmond, Washington, USA

Miraikan, Tokyo, Japan

MIT Museum, Cambridge, Massachusetts, USA

Museo de Informatica de la Republica Argentina, Buenos Aires, Argentina

National Museum of Computing History, Bletchley Park, Milton Keynes, UK

National Museum of Science and Technology, Madrid, Spain

Nexon Computer Museum, Jeju City, South Korea

Ontario Science Centre, Toronto, Canada

Rhode Island Computer Museum, Warwick, Rhode Island, USA

Samsung Innovation Museum, Suwon, South Korea

Science Centre NEMO, Amsterdam, The Netherlands

Science Museum, London, UK

Seoul Robot & AI Museum, Seoul, South Korea

Shanghai Science and Technology Museum, Shanghai, China

Swedish National Museum of Science and Technology, Stockholm, Sweden

Swiss Museum of Computer Science, Digital Culture and Video Games (Musée Bolo), Lausanne, Switzerland

System Source Computer Museum, Hunt Valley, Maryland, USA

Podcasts

Changelog changelog.com

Security Now twit.tv

Software Engineering Radio se-radio.net

Spark with Nora Young cbc.ca

This Week in Tech twit.tv

University of Oxford podcasts.ox.ac.uk/series/computer-science

Websites

The Apple Museum theapplemuseum.org

HP Computer Museum hpmuseum.net

IBM Archives ibm.com/history

Doug Engelbart Institute dougengelbart.org

Steve Jobs Archive stevejobsarchive.com

Khan Academy khanacademy.org

NASA nasa.gov

World Wide Web Consortium w3.org

Konrad Zuse Internet Archive zuse.zib.de

INDEX

3D printer 78
@ symbol 60

A
abacus 6, 10, 12
AI assistant 102, 117
Airbnb 61, 98
algorithm 23–25, 36–37, 43, 48, 50–51, 53, 68–71, 77, 86, 89, 91, 104, 106, 117, 120–121, 125, 139
al-Jazari, Ismail 18
al-Khwarizmi 24
Allen, Frances 136
AlphaFold 115, 139
Altair 8800 64–65, 138
Altman, Sam 139
Amazon 94, 103, 107
analog computing 11, 13, 26–27, 35, 133
Analytical Engine 20–21, 23, 43, 132
Android, operating system 57, 65, 75, 97
Anonymous, hacking group 92
Antikythera Mechanism 11, 13, 26
app 79, 82–83, 97–99, 107, 112–113, 118, 122, 128, 139
Apple Inc. 57, 63–64, 67, 72–73, 75, 79, 84, 91, 97, 99, 103, 107, 137–138
application, computer 21, 60, 79, 91, 93, 97, 122–123
architecture, computer 8, 37, 59, 73, 133–134, 137
Arithmometer (calculator) 21
ARPANET 58–60, 136, 137
artificial general intelligence (AGI) 71, 128
artificial intelligence (AI) 6–7, 18, 33, 47, 53, 70–71, 74–75, 77, 86, 88, 97, 102, 104–105, 107, 109, 111, 113, 115–118, 122–124, 128–130, 135, 137, 139
artificial neural network (ANN) 53, 105
assembly language 48, 51
astrolabe 6, 13
Atari 2600 66
ATLAS, robot 109
AT&T 57, 61
automata 18–19
autonomy 7, 32–33, 38, 76, 108–109
AV (autonomous vehicle) 76–77, 85
Aztecs 12

B
Babbage, Charles 20–21, 23, 25, 29, 53, 132
Babylonian mathematics 13
backpropagation 105, 137
Bacon, Francis 16–17, 26
battery 7, 82, 97, 107
Bell, Alexander Graham 28, 42, 45, 54, 57, 134–136
Berners-Lee, Tim 80–81, 88, 138
Big Data 112–113
binary code 16–17, 25, 31, 37, 42, 44, 46, 48–49, 53, 105, 110–111, 123, 127
biometric data 106
bit 6, 9–10, 36, 40, 46, 52, 65, 69, 79, 82, 91, 110–111, 126, 130
Bitcoin 100–101
Bletchley Park 36, 41
blockchain 101, 114
Bluetooth 31, 82, 99
Bombe 41–42
Boolean operations 25, 35, 38–39, 44, 51, 123, 132, 135
Boole, George 25, 38, 132
Boston Dynamics 109
Brin, Sergey 88–89, 138, 139
Bush, Vannevar 35, 38, 63, 80, 133, 135
business intelligence 96
Butterfly Effect 56
byte 46

C
calculator 10, 12, 15, 20–21, 38, 97
camera 8, 77
cameras 7–8, 74, 77, 84, 97, 113
carbon emissions 125, 127
cartridge, ROM 66
CD (Compact Disc) 87
central processing unit (CPU) 8–9, 21, 42, 50
Cerf, Vinton 59, 136–137
CGI (computer-generated imagery) 74–75
chatbot 129
chatbots 47, 70
ChatGPT-4 47, 116
Chinese Room Argument 70, 128
Chromebooks 57
Clockwork 14
COBOL 44, 134
codebreakers 40–41
Colossus 41–43, 45, 134
Commodore 64 66
compiler 48, 134, 136
computer bug 44, 120, 122
computer modelling 56
computer science 6–7, 37, 39, 51, 70, 74, 96, 139
Computing Machinery and Intelligence 47
consciousness upload 126
constants 120
contactless technology 107
CPU (central processing unit) 54
cracker 52
Cray 1, supercomputer 65
cryptocurrency 100
crypto mining 74, 96, 101, 128, 134
cybercriminal 52, 61
cybernetics 33

D
DARPA (Defense Advanced Research Projects Agency) 108
Dartmouth Workshop 70, 102
data 6–10, 19–20, 24–25, 28–29, 31, 37, 42–44, 46, 50, 53, 56–58, 60, 67–68, 71, 76–77, 79–83, 87–89, 91, 93, 95–96, 98–99, 102, 104–107, 109–110, 112–113, 116–123, 125–128, 131, 133, 137
databases 123
da Vinci, Leonardo 18
debugging 44, 51, 122
decimal code 16–17, 46, 49
decision tree 105
Deep Blue, chess computer 86
deepfake 124
DeepMind 115
desktop, virtual 63
Difference Engine 20
differential analyzer 35, 37
Diffie-Hellman key exchange 68
Diffie, Whitfield 68–69, 137
Digesting Duck 18
digital code 8, 13
display 9, 32, 34, 62–63, 66–67, 72, 81, 84–85, 87
distributed network 59, 101
DoS (denial of service) 92
Drive 9, 103
DVD (Digital Versatile Disc) 87

E
Easley, Annie 136
e-commerce 85
Edison, Thomas 28, 31, 44, 133
education 129, 133, 139
EDVAC (Electronic Discrete Variable Automatic Computer) 48
e-ink 87
electromagnet 22
electromagnetic relay 22, 44
electromechanical computer 27
email 57, 59–61, 79, 93, 97, 117, 125, 131
encryption 68–69, 131, 137
Engelbart, Douglas 62–63, 135
ENIAC (Electronic Numerical Integrator and Computer) 43, 45, 48–49, 54, 56
Enigma code 40–42
e-reader 87
Ethereum 100–101
Euclid 25
exoskeletons 109, 115

F
Facebook 84, 95, 127, 139
Fairchild Channel F 66
Fairchild Semiconductor 55, 57
Fancy Bear 92
Fitbit 99
Fleming, John 31, 133
floppy diskettes 50, 72
flowchart 24, 36, 120
Flowers, Tommy 41–42, 134
Fortran 51, 136
fractal 56
freedom of speech 130
functional language 123
fuzzy logic 77, 105

G
Galileo Galilei 14
Gates, Bill 65, 73, 138
General Data Protection Regulations (GDPR) 110
general intelligence 71, 128
generative AI 7, 104, 109, 116–117, 130, 137, 139
germanium 45
gire control systems 27
GNU Project 75
Google 76, 83, 88–89, 97, 103, 107,

115, 137–139
GPS (Global Positioning System) 76–77, 82–83, 108, 135
GPT (Generative Pre-trained Transformer) 116
graphical user interface 62, 135
GUI 62–63, 73, 135

H

hackers 52, 61, 103, 122, 131
hallucination, AI 117
Hamilton, Margaret 136
Hansen Writing Ball 27
haptics 108
hard disk drive (HDD) 50
hard drive 9
hardware 7, 23, 44, 48, 57, 64, 73, 76, 102–103, 111, 118, 123
Harvard Mark II 44
Hassabis, Demis 139
headphones 9
hexadecimal code 10
Hinton, Geoffrey 137
Hollerith, Herman 6, 29, 133
Hollerith Tabulating Machine 6
home area network (HAN) 113
Homebrew Computer Club 64, 66, 72
Hopper, Grace 44, 48, 134
HTML (HyperText Markup Language) 81
human computers 30
Huygens, Christiaan 14
hyperlink 35, 81

I

IBM (International Business Machines) 6, 29, 48–49, 51, 56–57, 70, 72–73, 86, 102, 107, 133, 136
I Ching 16
iCloud 103
icons 63, 84, 97
Imitation Game 47
Industrial Revolution 20
input device 8
Instagram 95, 139
Intel 57
Internet 6, 28, 58–61, 68, 76, 80–81, 88–91, 93, 95, 97–98, 103, 108, 110, 112–113, 125, 127, 129, 136–137
Internet of Things (IoT) 112–113
Internet service provider (ISP) 103, 127, 131
iPhone 67, 97, 138
iPod 91

J

Jacquard, Joseph 19–21, 23, 29
Jacquard loom 19–21, 23
Jobs, Steve 63–64, 73, 91, 97, 137, 138

K

Kahn, Robert 59, 136–137
Kelvin tide predictor 26, 35
keyboard 8, 27, 67
Kilby, Jack 54

L

laptop 64, 72, 79
large language model 47, 117
laser 10, 76–78, 87, 111, 127
Lawson, Jerry 64, 66
LCD, liquid crystal display 34, 72
LEDs (light-emitting diodes) 34
Leibniz, Gottfried 16–17, 132
lidar 77
Linux operating system 57, 75, 97
logic language 123
loudspeaker 9, 107, 112
Lovelace, Ada 23, 25, 53, 132

M

machine code 48, 51, 134
machine learning 7, 53, 71, 101–102, 104–106, 112, 114–115, 123
Magnavox Odyssey 66
mainframes 48–49, 51, 54, 59–60, 73, 80, 103
malware 60–61, 131
Manchester Mark 1 48
Manhattan Project 35, 133
MANIAC 56
Marconi, Guglielmo 31–32, 92, 133
Mayan numeral system 12–13, 71
Mechanical Knight 18
mechanical servants 18
meme, Internet 95
Memex, memory extension 35, 63, 80
memory 9, 21, 35, 42, 46, 50, 54, 65–66, 95, 112, 132
Mercury delay line 43
Mersenne prime 68
Metaverse 84
microchip 9, 50, 54–55, 57, 65, 74, 111, 123
microcomputer 64–65
microfabrication 55
microphone 8
Microsoft 57, 65, 73, 75, 79, 103, 116, 138

Microsoft Office 79
Millennium Bug 44
MIT (Massachusetts Institute of Technology) 35, 38–39, 52, 60–61, 69, 75, 87, 102, 109, 133–138
modem 42
monitor, computer 9
Moore, Gordon 57, 64
Moore's Law 57
Morse code 22, 31, 92
motors 7, 32–33
mouse, computer 8, 62, 135
mp3 91
MS DOS 73

N

Nakamoto, Satoshi 101
Napier, John 15
Napier's "bones" 15
narrow AI 71, 77
NASA 30, 49, 84, 136
navigation 6, 82–83, 108
near-field technology 107
nepohualtzintzin (Aztec computer) 12
networks 28, 31, 42, 45, 58, 59, 137
Neuralink 114–115
NFT (non-fungible token) 114
Note G 23
Noyce, Robert 55, 57
NSA (National Security Agency) 41

O

object-oriented language 123
OneDrive 79, 103
online ethics 126
OpenAI 61, 116, 139
optical disc 9, 87
optical fiber 76
Osborne 1 72
oscillation 14
output device 8–9, 34, 67

P

packet switching 59
Page, Larry 88–89, 138–139
PageRank algorithm 89
PARC (Palo Alto Research Center) 63
Pascal, Blaise 15
Pascaline 15
password strength 17, 69
PC, IBM 72–73
pendulum 14
perceptron 53, 105
personal computer 7, 28, 34, 63, 66, 72–73, 80
photonics 127
phreaking 61
Playstations 57
printer 9
printer, inkjet 78
printer, laser 78
privacy 128
procedural language 123
program, life cycle 118
programming language 123
proof of stake 101
proof of work 101
pseudocode 120
punched card 19, 51, 133

Q

quantum computing 110–111, 131
quaternions 75
qubit 110–111

R

radar 45, 77, 133, 135–136
Radio Shack 72
radio waves 31–32, 45, 64, 82–83, 90–92, 107, 111, 133
RAM (random access memory) 9, 50
reality–virtuality continuum 84
robot 7, 9, 18, 24, 32–33, 93, 108–109, 115, 130
robot arm 33
robotaxis 76–77
ROM (read-only memory) 54
RSA algorithm 68–69

S

sand timers 14
satellite Internet 129
scanner 8
scientific hooligan 92
Scientific Method 16
scripting language 123
search engine 88–89
Searle, John 70–71
sensor 8, 33
sensors 7, 33, 77, 108–109, 113
SETI (Search for Extraterrestrial Intelligence) 64
Shannon, Claude 35, 38–39, 46, 135
shannon, unit 46
Shockley, William 45, 54–55, 134
silicon 35, 45, 54, 64, 134
Silicon Valley 35, 54, 64, 134
Sinclair Spectrum 66

Skype 93
smartphone 6, 9, 13, 63, 67, 74, 82–83, 91, 97–99, 106–107, 111–112
smart speaker 8, 107
smartwatch 8, 99
social media 24, 94–95, 130, 139
software 7, 23, 44, 52, 57, 60–61, 64, 65–66, 73, 75, 79–80, 85, 88, 118–120, 122–123, 126, 131, 134, 136, 138–139
software testing 122
solid-state memory 9
Sony Playstation 66
spintronics 127
Spot, robot 109
storage, computer 8–9, 21, 26, 43, 46, 49–50, 65, 79, 87, 91, 103
suanpan (Chinese abacus) 10, 12
supercomputer 35, 65
superintelligence 124
supervised machine learning 105

T

tablet computer 67
TCP/IP 59, 136–137
Tech Model Railroad Club 52
Technological Singularity 124
telegraph 17, 22, 28, 31, 38, 41, 44
telephone 28, 38, 42, 44, 57–59, 61, 76, 82, 93, 97, 137
telepresence 93
Teletext 62
television 34
Texas Instruments 54
The Cloud 9
thermionic triode 45
thermionic valve 31
Three Laws of Robotics 33
TikTok 95
Tomlinson, Ray 60
touchscreen 8, 67, 97
TRADIC 54
Traitorous Eight 55, 57
transistor 28, 45, 53–55, 57, 127, 134
transistors 6, 17, 45, 49, 54–55, 57
Trojan Horse 61
Turing, Alan 7–8, 36–38, 40–42, 47–48, 70–71, 135–137
Turing Test 47, 70, 135
turtle robots 33
"twofold instrument" 17

U

Uber 76, 98
Uncanny Valley 130

Unimate, robot arm 33
UNIVAC I 49
Unix 57, 61, 75, 79
unsupervised machine learning 105, 115

V

vacuum tubes 8, 34, 49, 54
variables 35, 51, 120
virtual machine 7–8, 36–37
virtual reality (VR) 84, 108
virtual wallet 107
virus, computer 60–61, 92, 96, 131
VoIP (Voice over Internet Protocol) 93
von Neumann, John 37–38, 102, 133
VPN (virtual private network) 103
VR headsets 84, 99

W

Walter, William Gray 33, 45, 53
water clocks 14
Watson, Thomas 28–29, 48, 102, 107
Waymo 76
wearable technology 99, 113
West, Gladys 135
WhatsApp 95, 139
Wi-Fi 17, 31, 90–91, 129
WikiLeaks 92
Wikipedia 95
Windows operating system 57, 73, 79, 138
World Wide Web 7, 28, 35, 59, 62, 80–82, 88, 108, 138
worm, computer 61
Wozniak, Steve 63–64, 137, 138

X

X 95
Xerox 63
Xerox Alto 63

Y

YouTube 95, 127

Z

zero 12–13, 101
Zuckerberg, Mark 95, 139
Zuse, Konrad 38, 134

© 2024 Shelter Harbor Press.

All rights reserved. No part of this publication may be reproduced, stored in a retrieval system, or transmitted, in any form or by any means, electronic, mechanical, photocopying, recording, or otherwise, without prior written permission from the publisher.

Cataloging-in-Publication Data has been applied for and may be obtained from the Library of Congress.

ISBN 978-1-62795-200-2

Series Concept and Direction: Jeanette Limondjian
Design: Bradbury and Williams
Copy editors: Meredith MacArdle, Stevie Derrick
Proofreader: Julia Adams
Picture Research: Clare Newman
Consultant: Dr. Peter Bennett
Cover Design: Igor Satanovsky

Publisher's Note: While every effort has been made to ensure that the information herein is complete and accurate, the publishers and authors make no representations or warranties either expressed or implied of any kind with respect to this book to the reader. Neither the authors nor the publisher shall be liable or responsible for any damage, loss, or expense of any kind arising out of information contained in this book. The thoughts or opinions expressed in this book represent the personal views of the authors and not necessarily those of the publisher. Further, the publisher takes no responsibility for third party websites or their content.

Shelter Harbor Press
603 West 115th Street Suite 163
New York, New York 10025

For further information please contact
info@shelterharborpress.com

Printed and bound in China.

10 9 8 7 6 5 4 3 2 1

PICTURE CREDITS

Front Cover
Shutterstock: Marko Aliaksandr main image, Everett Collection background.
Endpapers
Shutterstock: Everett Collection

BOOK
Alamy: Alpha Historical 30, Anthony David Baynes 62tl, Fotan 109t, Glasshouse Images 42, Patrick Guenette 68t, Maximum fil 74, Naeblys 115tr, PA Images 34, Photo 12 31b, Pictorial Press Ltd 28, PJF Military Collection 41t, Prisma Archivo 50cr, Science History Images 37, 48-49, Sueddeutsche Zeitung Photo 32, 50b, White House Photo 93, World History Archive 22b, **Bradbury & Williams**: original source image Alamy: Odoroaga Monica 77cr; **Library of Congress**: 133 top right; **NOAA**: 82bl; **Roy Williams**: 36b; **Shutterstock**: 4HPH4 89b, A Pisit Hrpp 90, All is Magic 53, Ambrosiniv 41b, Apisorn 124tl, Asharkyu 2-3, 76, Svetlana Avv 112, Carlos E. Azevedo 91, Gualtiero Boffi 92, Paolo Bona 138tr, Buffalo Boy 100t, CKA 108, Drsera 80, Everett Collection 24-25b, 56tr, Feng Yu 61t, Frame Stock Footage 125, Franticoo 67, Gorodenkoff 77tl, 84, 107, 113, 131, Gorynvd 129tr, Evgeny Haritonov 130b, Steve Heao 127bl, I Wei Huang 26, Huticon 96, I am Z Mai 101tr, I M Imagery 55b, Tim Jenner 20, Max Kegfire 126b, Fredereick Legrand-COMEO 139tr, LuchschenF 127tr, Jacob Lund 94, M Disk 116, M Disk 5tcl, Macro Vector 85tl, Makhh 83, Maryia_K 130tl, Artie Medredev 101bl, Monkey Business Media 128bl, Nico El Nino 7b, 117b, 129b, Petertimea Design 126tr, Pluie_r 89tl, Andrey Popov 99, Olga Popova 133br, Marley Pug 97bl, Raigvi 54, Raw Cap Photo 78tl, R-Bue 78br, Tapati Rinchumrus 103b, Roibu 86, Sdx15 102, Siberian Art 103tr, Nadiq Snopek 114, Sp3n 106, Stock-Asso 70, 128tr, Studio Molekuul 115bl, Studio Light & Shade 120br, Gregorz Sulkowski 19, Sundry Photographs 88tr, Tada Images 117cl, Tricky Shark 98, Urban Space 7t, 109b, Vallabh Soni 111t, Vchal 71tr, Bartlomeij K. Wroblewski 111b; **The Wellcome Library, London**: 132bl, 132tr; **Wikipedia**: CC BY 2.0 6b, 29, 35, 57, 62br, 95, 137tr, 139br, CC BY-SA 2.0 73b 139tl, CC BY-SA 2.0 DE 135bl, CC BY-SA 2.0 FR 65, 136tl, CC BY 2.5 11, 47, CC BY SA 2.5 6t, 12bl, 13, 51, CC BY 3.0 5tr, 72, 87tl, 97tr, 134tr, 137tl, CC BY-SA 3.0 10, 12br, 64, 75tl, 88bl, 134br, 135tr, 136br, 137br, 138tl, 138br, CC BY-SA 3.0 FR 4bl, 15bl, CC BY-SA 4.0 4tr, 15tr, 23tr, 27b, 33b, 39, 40, 55cr, 61b, 87br, 132br, 137bl, 138bl, 139bl, CC0 1.0 38, 85br, GNU Free Documentation License 27t, 45t, Public Domain incl. U.S. 14, 16, 17tl, 18bl, 18tr, 21, 22cl, 23b, 31t, 33t, 36t, 43cr, 43br, 44, 52, 56bl, 58, 60tl, 63, 66, 73tr, 75br, 79, 82tr, 100b, 135tl, 136tr, 136bl.
Bradbury and Williams: 8–9, 17, 24t, 25t, 37b, 39, 45b, 4959, 60b, 68b, 69b, 71b, 81, 104, 105, 119, 120bl 121, 122, 123.

TIMELINES
Alamy: Anthony David Baynes; **CERN**; **Library of Congress**; **NASA**; **Roy Williams**; **Shutterstock**: Alice Photo, Guartiero Boff, Fred Duval, Everett Collection, Gorodenkoff, Tim Jenner, Alessia Pierdomemio, Roibu, Tada Images; **Wellcome Library, London**; **Wikipedia**: CC BY 2.0, CC BY-SA 2.0, CC BY 2.5, CC BY-SA 2.5, CC BY 3.0, CC BY-SA 3.0, CC BY-SA 3.0 FR, CC BY-SA 4.0, CC0 1.0, OGL 2, Public Domain incl, U.S.

REVERSE TIMELINE
Alamy: Classic Stock, Klaus Ohlenschlaeger, Stefan Sollfors, Hugh Threlfall, Trek and Shoot, Zoonar GmbH; **Shutterstock**: Charnsitr, Cincila, Oleg Gawvilo FF; **Wikipedia**: CC BY-SA 2.0, CC BY-SA 2.1, CC BY 3.0, CC BY-SA 3.0, Public Domain incl, U.S.

Publisher's note: Every effort has been made to trace copyright holders and seek permission to use illustrative material. The publishers wish to apologize for any inadvertent errors or omissions and would be glad to rectify these in future editions.

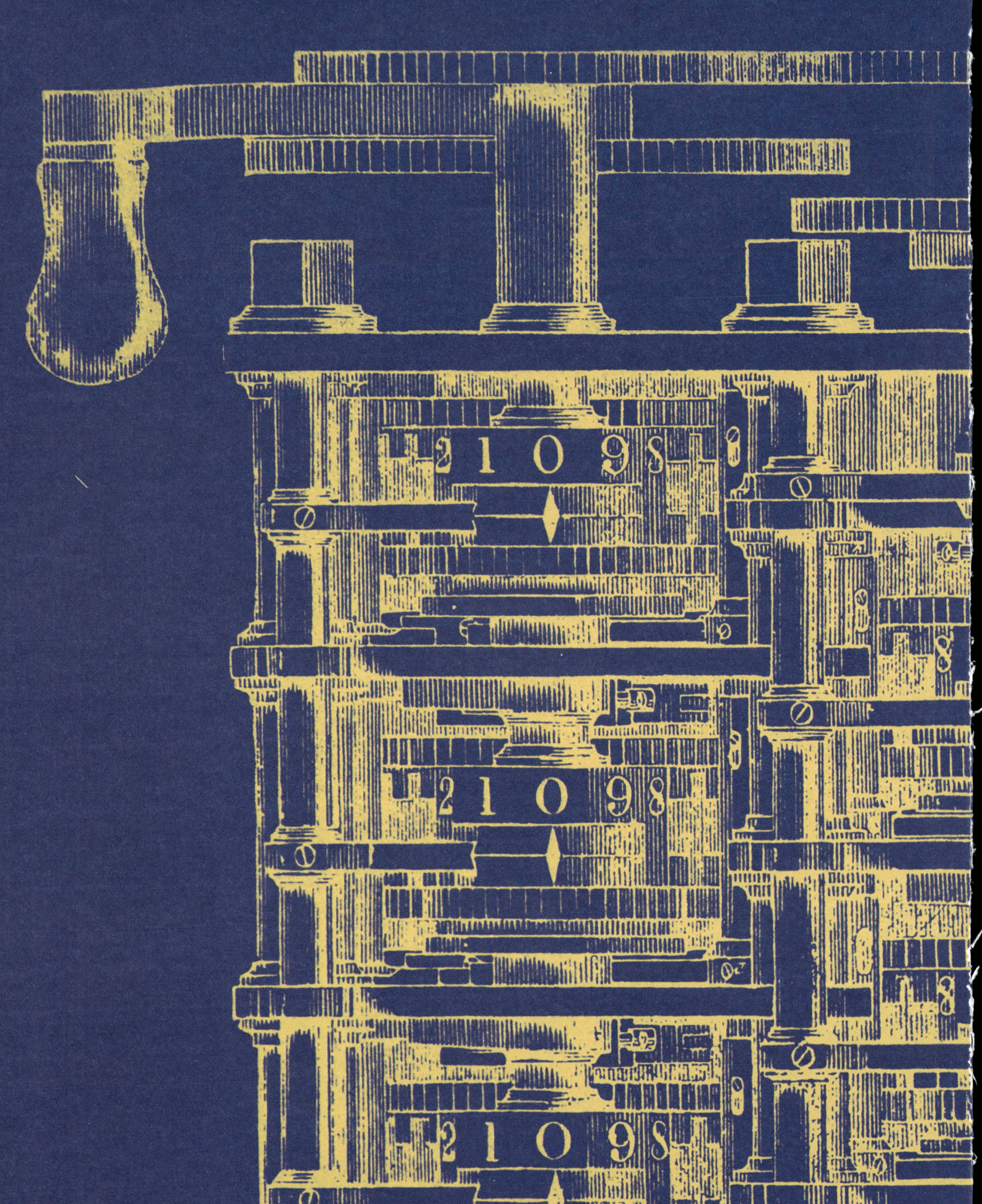